YOU ARE NOT A CODE

Rebuilding Identity and Community

In an Age of Diagnosis

Shannon Lea Sinnett

DEDICATION

This book is dedicated to the many people who have walked with me through trials and tribulations, those who helped sharpen me as iron sharpens iron.

To my mother and father, who laid the foundation of community in my life from the very beginning. Through their example, I learned that resilience, accountability, and connection are built in relationships long before any system attempts to define them.

Above all, I acknowledge God and the Holy Spirit, who allowed me to walk the long road of wisdom, knowledge, learning, and experience. Through every hardship, every lesson, and every season of growth, His guidance shaped the path that led to this work.

Second only to God and the Holy Spirit are my three sons, whose insight, wisdom, patience, and love have supported me through every misstep, challenge, and season of growth along the way.

To the friends who endured spiritual hardships beside me and grew through those seasons with faith, perseverance, and truth.

The mentors, teachers, and learning experiences through college, the mental health system, and every difficult lesson along the way strengthened understanding and shaped wisdom.

To the clients who trusted me with their stories and allowed me to walk beside them in their struggles. Their courage, honesty, and resilience shaped my understanding of people as much as any education ever could.

Moreover, to the many individuals and families who opened their homes to me and shared their cultures, stories, and lives. Through neighbors, elders, friends, and even those who once felt like enemies.

I learned what it truly means to build resilience, identity, and community.

This book exists because of those relationships.

WHO THIS BOOK IS FOR

This book is for those who sense that something important has been lost in our culture. It is for individuals who recognize that human identity cannot be reduced to categories, symptoms, or codes.

This is for parents, mentors, community leaders, and educators committed to rebuilding the relational foundations that help individuals grow through hardship.

It is also for psychologists, mental health counselors, social workers, and other professionals who serve individuals facing emotional and psychological struggles. Clinical care plays a critical and necessary role in treating severe mental illness and stabilizing individuals in crisis. Clinical systems were designed primarily to diagnose, assess, and treat impairment.

They were never intended to replace the relational environments where identity, character, and resilience are formed. Understanding that distinction protects both the profession and the people it serves.

This book is also written for college students and emerging professionals entering fields such as counseling, psychology, social work, ministry, and community leadership. Many will spend years studying theories, diagnostic frameworks, and institutional systems. Those frameworks have value, but they must be understood within the broader context of human development and community life.

- Human beings are not formed solely by systems.

- Identity develops through belonging.

- Resilience grows through experience.

- Wisdom is shaped through relationships.

For this reason, colleges preparing students for helping professions should consider the importance of evaluating not only academic preparation, but also relational maturity, life experience, and understanding of community.

Churches also play a vital role. Long before modern systems existed, faith communities were places where individuals found guidance, mentorship, accountability, and belonging. When these roles weaken, individuals often turn to institutions to fill needs that were once addressed through discipleship and community.

This book is also for clients and patients navigating clinical systems who are seeking clarity about what they truly need to grow and heal.

Clinical treatment can stabilize symptoms, but many individuals are also searching for guidance, mentorship, accountability, purpose, and community. Understanding the difference between clinical treatment and relational support empowers individuals to pursue the resources that will truly strengthen their lives.

If we are to support individuals and families well, we must understand the distinction between clinical care and the relational environments where people learn to grow.

This book invites readers to reconsider that distinction and to rediscover the role that community, mentorship, accountability, and purpose play in shaping human identity.

If these questions matter to you, then this conversation is for you.

Why This Book Matters

Healthy societies once depended on several distinct systems working together: community, church, education, and clinical care. Each served a different purpose in forming individuals and strengthening relationships.

Today, those boundaries are becoming blurred.

Clinical mental health systems are increasingly asked to help individuals form identity, relationships, and purpose, even though those responsibilities were never the original function of clinical care. Mental health systems were designed to stabilize severe psychological impairment, not to replace the role of the community in shaping human development.

At the same time, many churches have shifted toward programs, entertainment, and therapeutic-style sermons, rather than focusing on discipleship, spiritual accountability, and relational mentorship. When the church becomes program-driven instead of relationship-driven, it can unintentionally lose its role in forming spiritually mature individuals.

Educational systems also reflect this shift. Schools and universities often prioritize credentials, career preparation, and financial outcomes, while giving far less attention to personal development, self-awareness, or equipping individuals to discern whether a particular career path truly fits their character, strengths, and calling. The result is that individuals are increasingly shaped by institutions rather than relationships.

Instead of being formed through families, mentors, elders, and communities, many people search for identity and belonging within systems that were never designed to provide them.

When these boundaries collapse, every system begins carrying responsibilities it was never designed to hold. For instance:

- Clinical care becomes overwhelmed.

- Churches become program-driven.

- Education produces credentials without formation.

- Communities slowly disappear.

Individuals are left searching for purpose, identity, and belonging in places that cannot fully provide them.

This book exists because restoring these boundaries may be essential not only for the health of our institutions, but for the health of our relationships, families, and communities.

CULTURE WARNING

Our culture has begun treating nearly every human struggle as a mental health disorder. In doing so, we have slowly forgotten the role that families, mentors, elders, and communities once played in forming resilient individuals.

Clinical mental health care is essential for severe psychological impairment. However, it cannot replace the community's work in shaping identity, purpose, and belonging.

Sociologists have documented a steady collapse of community life. Robert Putnam describes how civic engagement, local relationships, and social participation have dramatically declined in modern society (Putnam, 2000).

Psychological research confirms the consequences of this shift. Humans are wired for connection, and prolonged isolation is strongly linked to depression, anxiety, and declining health (Cacioppo & Cacioppo, 2018; Holt-Lunstad, Smith, & Layton, 2010). The U.S. Surgeon General has recently identified loneliness and social isolation as a growing public health crisis (U.S. Surgeon General, 2023).

At the same time, everyday human struggles are increasingly filtered through clinical and diagnostic language.

Sociologists call this the medicalization of society, where experiences once addressed through relationships, mentorship, or community guidance are now defined as medical problems (Conrad, 2007; Conrad & Barker, 2010).

The result is a culture fixated on symptoms while becoming increasingly disconnected in its relationships.

Long before modern sociology and psychology described these patterns, Scripture warned of a similar cultural drift. The Apostle Paul wrote that in difficult times, people would become "lovers of themselves," increasingly disconnected from one another and from the relational bonds that once held families and communities together (2 Timothy 3:1–5).

When relationships weaken and community collapses, individuals begin searching for belonging in systems that were never designed to provide it.

Clinical mental health systems were never intended to replace the role of the community.

However, as the community disappears, those systems are increasingly asked to carry responsibilities they were never designed to hold.

When the boundary between clinical care and human development collapses, both systems suffer:

- Clinical care becomes overwhelmed.

- Community disappears.

- Families fractured.

- Isolation grows.

We slowly forget how human beings are meant to form identity, resilience, and a sense of belonging.

The collapse of the community is forcing clinical systems to carry the burden of human development.

TABLE OF CONTENTS

INTRODUCTION

This book argues that while clinical mental health care is essential for severe impairment and crisis, our culture has increasingly medicalized normal human struggle. In doing so, we have blurred the boundary between illness and identity, often replacing community, mentorship, and relational resilience with diagnostic labels and symptom management.

What was once understood as part of human experience, grief, hardship, identity formation, and personal growth are now frequently interpreted through the language of pathology. As a result, struggles that were once navigated through relationships, accountability, wisdom, and community are increasingly redirected into systems designed primarily to manage symptoms and reduce risk.

Clinical care has an important and necessary role. When individuals face severe psychological distress, psychiatric intervention and structured treatment can be lifesaving. This book does not reject that reality.

However, clinical systems were never designed to replace community, mentorship, family wisdom, or the relational processes through which identity is formed.

When the line between illness and normal human struggle blurs, an unintended consequence emerges ordinary life difficulties come to be viewed through diagnostic rather than developmental or relational frameworks.

The result is a cultural shift.

Community weaknesses.

Mentorship disappears.

Relational resilience declines.

Institutions expand to fill the gap.

The solution is not the rejection of clinical care, but the restoration of discernment, the ability to clearly distinguish between true psychiatric disorder and the ordinary human need for belonging, growth, accountability, and connection.

Human beings are not primarily diagnostic problems to be managed.

They are relational beings whose identities are shaped by experience, responsibility, community, and meaning.

When these foundations weaken, systems attempt to compensate.

However, systems cannot replace what relationships were designed to build.

This book explores how we arrived at this cultural shift and how communities can begin rebuilding the relational foundations that sustain resilience, identity, and long-term stability.

Because before we assign a code, we must remember something fundamental:

You are not a code

BRIDGE TO CHAPTER 1

Understanding how we reached this point requires looking beyond theory and systems. It requires looking at how people grow, struggle, and form identity within the environments that shape them.

Before I studied counseling in a classroom, I was learning about people in living rooms, neighborhoods, and communities where real life unfolded.

My understanding of human struggle did not begin in institutions.

It began in the community.

That is where the story starts.

PART 1

BUILT BY COMMUNITY NOT INSTITUTION

CHAPTER 1

BEFORE THE SYSTEM

I grew up in Springfield, Ohio, in a chaotic but resilient neighborhood, where thirty kids played outside until dark. We fought. We made up. We learned about culture. We learned resilience. Everyone knew everyone else's business. We all had various levels of income and nationality. We were in a diverse neighborhood.

My parents loved each other but fought daily. My brother and I fought constantly. We were always in trouble. I call this building resilience.

There were no diagnoses. We talked about problems.

We experimented, we got our butts whipped, we wrote in diaries. We processed life together.

Community shaped identity long before any system did.

We are all called and have different gifts in this world, but it is all about serving.

Educational institutions, such as schools and colleges, were established to prepare us for participation in an industrial society.

I never fit into that system.

I quit school in fifth grade.

It made no sense to me.

However, I was never without education.

I had friends from everywhere. Some stayed at my place.

At fourteen, I worked as a hostess in a Greek restaurant. I was a social butterfly. If I walked into a store, I had to learn about the people there. I was always studying human behavior without realizing it.

My confidence formed early.

It did not come from grades.

It came from interaction.

My parents were independent people. They loved each other deeply, but conflict was constant.

My brother and I fought often.

We were always in trouble.

Nevertheless, we also learned accountability.

We faced consequences.

We did not escape from conflict.

Conflict did not weaken us. It strengthened us.

The curriculum did not provide instruction on resilience. This is the result of firsthand experience.

In those days, we had diaries.

My girlfriends wrote in mine.

If there was a fight, it went into the diary.

If there was heartbreak, it went into the diary.

We did things to make each other laugh.

We would go through drive-thrus and order the wrong food, throw eggs at houses, prank-call our teachers, put crazy makeup on our mothers, and knock on doors before running away.

Innocent things

Long before clinical language entered our lives, we processed emotion together. Even when others called us names, we created our own identities to remind ourselves that those labels were not true. When we were ridiculed, we developed resilience and emotional stability by learning to cope with rejection.

We wrote letters in school, gave each other nicknames, and encouraged one another. It was communication, expression, and belonging. No one called it therapy. It was simply a community.

When I reflect, it is clear that identity took shape through connections with others rather than through labels or categories. It is formed through playful antics, enjoyment, and bold exploration.

As I moved from Springfield to North Hill and then to Kenmore, I experienced diverse cultures. One community centered around church and family. Another revolved around parties and chaos. Kenmore introduced drugs, fighting, and darker influences.

I was naïve in many ways. I did not yet understand the depth of trauma my friends were carrying. Certain individuals had suffered mistreatment. Some of those struggles stemmed from alcoholism. Some individuals suffered profound wounds.

As we got older, I began to hear their stories. When people are young, they rarely reveal experiences of abuse, molestation, or rape. These realities often remain secret. As we matured, my friends began sharing things they believed I had been too immature to understand earlier. They assumed I would reject or disbelieve what had happened to them because those things had never happened to me.

What I did understand was this: no two people carried the same story.

That awareness would later shape how I viewed diagnosis.

When I moved to Michigan before turning eighteen, I entered another world. I held jobs at JCPenney, in customer service, and at a dentist's office, where I almost fainted during a procedure and did not return after lunch.

Eventually, I worked at a country club. I met wealthy professionals and leaders. Money did not intimidate me. What became clear was that people with resources experienced loneliness just as much as everyone else.

Eventually, I began cleaning homes.

That is where my real counseling education began.

In kitchens and bathrooms, people tell their stories. I met people from every kind of struggle:

- Lonely individuals

- Divorcing couples

- Elders facing decline

- Families in crisis

I prayed with people.

I listened

I advocated

I observed patterns.

Most of all, I built relationships with people and families.

No DSM

No codes

No billing structures

Just stories

Nearly every client eventually asked me about their life.

I encountered suffering across every economic level.

I witnessed that wealth did not remove pain. Over time, a pattern emerged: loneliness did not discriminate.

Others held me accountable.

Others listened to me.

We shared life.

Over time, I realized something profound: most people do not need classification first. They need to be heard.

For twenty-five years, I served doctors, teachers, business owners, atheists, Christians, gay couples, elders, and families of every background.

I saw:

- Elder abuse

- Hoarding

- Collapsing marriages

- Suicidal thoughts

- Isolation

- Addiction

There was no single pattern. No single code. No single label that explains humanity.

They do not teach you this in a degree program. They teach you systems. They teach you frameworks. They teach you documentation.

Nevertheless, working in people's homes teaches empathy, understanding, cultural awareness, different ways of living, and the ability to see life from another perspective. It teaches you to share in people's hurts, pains, and struggles.

Looking back on my childhood, I ask a question I believe we should all ask:

What did your childhood teach you about resilience?

Mine taught me independence. It taught me consequences. It taught me that energy is not disorder, and development does not happen on a fixed timeline.

If my brother and I had been clinically assessed at certain moments, we would have received labels. We were energetic. We struggled to sit still. Our attention did not fit a classroom mold.

However, development and disorder are not always the same thing. Not every high-energy child is dysfunctional. Not every delayed learner is impaired. Sometimes maturity arrives later. Sometimes intelligence expresses itself differently.

God made us different.

The structure of institutions often requires categorization. However, childhood is not always meant to conform to structure.

Over the years, I also saw the other side:

families deeply embedded in medical systems. A pill for sleep. A pill for anxiety. A pill for blood pressure.

Medication has its place. I am not against it.

However, medication is often meant to be a temporary stabilization, not a permanent identity.

There is a difference between:

Healthy grief

Temporary depression

Normal anxiety

Clinical mental illness

If we do not learn to distinguish between the two, we risk medicating development rather than strengthening resilience.

If my childhood had been evaluated through a checklist, I might have been labeled.

Nevertheless, I was not broken.

I was becoming.

What built me was not structure, documentation, or classification. It was conflict, culture, freedom, consequence, faith, and relationship.

That is the education that formed my lens.

Before I ever entered a classroom to study counseling, I was already studying people.

Before I learned diagnostic language, I learned how to sit with someone's pain.

Before I understood treatment plans, I understood belonging.

Community shaped me long before the system ever tried to.

So, when I later entered a world that required categories before connection, something inside me resisted.

That resistance would change the direction of my life.

CHAPTER 2

LEARNING PEOPLE IN LIVING ROOMS

Over the next twenty-five years, I would learn more about human struggle in living rooms than most textbooks could ever teach.

At fourteen, I worked in a Greek restaurant, learned how to relate culturally to Greeks, and learned that Greeks have high standards.

Working in the restaurant taught me how to serve others and relate to their needs, how to satisfy customers' needs, and how to have a good relationship with co-workers.

Later in Michigan, I worked at a country club, and eventually I began cleaning homes. I got bored and threw up a sign in the women's locker room to clean homes. I recall that the woman who intimidated me the most was also the first person to ask me to clean her house. She turned out to be the richest, most loving woman I ever served.

Cleaning homes became my real education in counseling. It became my children's transitional and growing environments.

They grew up learning about different environments and cultural upbringings with people who were not like them. Not once did I belittle my authority or title to put myself below anyone.

I remember a man who was married to a woman who was having an affair. He had tons of money, and the home was huge.

He sent me a FedEx letter after I stopped cleaning for his wife. I did not want to be in the middle of that situation, and she had not made my pay a priority.

In the letter, he wrote, "You are the only woman I have seen who smiles while cleaning toilets and still does an incredible job."

I believe if someone is going to call themselves a counselor, they should first learn how to study people outside an office.

Serve them.

Walk with them.

Eat with them.

See how they live.

Understand culture.

Observe family dynamics in real time.

Otherwise, it becomes easy to reduce someone to a chart, a symptom cluster, or a billing code.

For over twenty-five years, I worked in offices and homes across different communities. I met lawyers going through divorce. I met wealthy individuals who were deeply lonely and quietly suicidal. I encountered older adults who had lost their independence, vehicles, and financial control, now residing in ground-floor rooms or secluded care facilities.

I met seniors who felt forgotten. I met individuals who hoarded animals because they struggled to connect with people. I encountered countless marriage affairs rooted not in evil, but in unmet needs and poor communication. I observed addiction tied to grief, loneliness, regret, and unresolved pain.

I began to recognize cultural differences in eating habits, discipline, and family closeness. Cultures that remained connected across generations were less vulnerable to identity crises and despair. Not immune, but steadier.

I saw:

- Lawyers going through divorce.

- Lonely wealthy professionals

- Abandoned elders.

- Suicidal seniors

- Hoarding

- Abuse

- Affairs

- Addiction

- Cultural contrasts

In kitchens and bathrooms, people told me their stories.

I prayed with them

I listened

I advocated

No DSM

No codes

No billing

Just human connection

Over twenty-five years, I served doctors, teachers, business owners, gay couples, atheists, Christians, elders, and families from multiple cultures. I learned something simple: There is not one person in the world who does not struggle. Not every struggle is a disorder.

The predominant observations included identity confusion, loneliness, and diminished purpose. The people who seemed most stable were not the richest or the most educated.

They were the ones who could look back over their lives and feel they had lived with meaning, identity, and purpose. They had endured and felt satisfied with who they were.

Affairs often stemmed from a communication breakdown. Addiction was often about buried grief. Isolation was often about shame.

We were created for relationships. We were created with identity. We were created with purpose. Resilience has weakened in our culture. We say we want depression, suicide, and poverty to decline, but if we cannot discern between normal human pain and clinical illness, we risk over-medicalizing the human experience.

I have seen homes where medication stabilized a crisis. Moreover, I have seen homes where medication numbed emotion without addressing the root pain. I have seen individuals struggle to reconnect with themselves after years of suppressing feelings. Medication can be necessary. It can save lives. However, it cannot replace relationships, accountability, or identity work.

Cleaning homes taught me something profound about loneliness. Loneliness looks the same in a mansion as it does in a small apartment.

Wealth does not protect marriages. Education does not guarantee emotional maturity. Bigger homes do not equal a deeper connection.

The patterns were striking.

Successful women who appeared flawless in public would sit at their kitchen counters and cry when no one else was watching. They did not need a diagnosis. They needed someone to remind them that they did not have to perform an image daily. Many were exhausted from carrying marriages where their husbands were emotionally absent, physically unwell, or withdrawn. When they realized they were not alone when they heard that other marriages also struggled, something shifted. Shame loosened its grip.

Teenagers in stable neighborhoods felt oppressed in ways that were often unseen. They believed they were the only ones with divorced parents, conflict at home, or identity confusion. When I told them that what they were experiencing was common and survivable, relief would wash over them.

Sometimes all they needed was normalization and presence.

Over time, I began noticing patterns,

When people felt seen, their anxiety decreased.

When they were heard without judgment, their anger softened.

When someone believed in them, they became more capable.

Relief would wash over them.

Sometimes all they needed was normalization and presence.

Very few people needed a diagnosis first.

Most needed direction.

The language to express what they were feeling.

Someone steady enough to sit with discomfort.

What became clear was that families were consumed by busyness.

Parents run their children to sports and activities.

Careers are consuming marriages.

Schedules replacing conversation.

Connection slowly dissolved not from hatred, but from neglect.

It was common.

It was human.

It was repairable.

Inside institutions, distress is measured.

Inside homes, distress is lived.

In offices, symptoms are documented.

In living rooms, stories unfold.

In treatment plans, goals are written.

In kitchens, identity is rebuilt.

There were also moments when relational support was not enough. Severe psychiatric illness requires structured intervention. A crisis requires trained professionals. I am not blind to that reality. I have seen situations where immediate psychiatric care was necessary.

However, those cases were rare compared to the volume of ordinary human pain.

I remember one season when a close friend experienced severe fear and paranoia. They had been watching a lot of ISIS-related YouTube videos and started believing the things they were hearing.

 I was the first person they called.

Their family wanted to put him in an insane home. Everyone thought he was crazy and had lost his mind.

I prayed about it and tried to understand the root of what was happening. What I witnessed was fear.

He spent time at our house. I took him to church and explained to him that those videos had opened the door to a spirit of fear. After watching them, he began having bad dreams and believed we were being bombed. It was frightening.

Discernment was required.

Community support, spiritual grounding, and professional awareness all mattered.

Not every situation fits neatly into one category.

Sometimes intervention is layered, relationally, spiritually, and clinically, working together.

In this situation, the support he needed was relational and spiritual. God delivered him through the Word, but he had been in isolation, watching things he should not have been watching. It took someone he trusted to walk beside him and mentor him through that season.

To this day, he is completely normal and understands how easily we can let the wrong things into our minds when we isolate ourselves and expose ourselves to the wrong influences.

Discernment matters.

Over thousands of interactions across decades, the overwhelming pattern was this:

People wanted to be heard.

They wanted their story acknowledged.

They wanted direction.

They wanted to feel purposeful.

People often just need someone to listen to them and help them realize they are not crazy. We need others to communicate with, so our perspectives stay grounded. Human interaction helps keep our thoughts and behaviors in line.

Through connection with others, we remain accountable, balanced, and supported.

We were never meant to carry our thoughts alone. Relationships help us process life, challenge unhealthy thinking, and guide us back into clarity when fear, isolation, or confusion begin to take over.

Human connection is not optional; it is essential.

Many did not have one trusted friend they could speak to daily. Many were drowning in silence. Many needed someone to tell the truth and offer perspective.

I realized I carried a gift of trust. People told me things they had never told anyone. I spoke directly. I offered self-awareness. I did not prolong conversations unnecessarily. When people were ready to change, they changed quickly. Root issues surfaced faster than surface symptoms.

Medical systems often focus on symptom reduction. Relational systems focus on identity reconstruction.

Friendships take work.

Marriages take work.

Families take discipline.

Community requires resilience.

Medicine can stabilize a crisis.

However, vulnerability builds strength.

Control can look powerful. Vulnerability is stronger.

Another pattern I noticed was that most adults were never taught how to express their needs or emotions as children. Many were not taught accountability.

From a very young age, people are told not to cry, not to overreact, not to be dramatic, or not to "feel so much." Some were ignored when they needed comfort. Some were raised in homes where emotions were inconvenient or unsafe.

As adults, those same individuals struggled deeply in relationships.

I have sat with professionals, successful, educated, respected individuals who could not say a simple sentence like, "I feel hurt," or "I need reassurance." Instead, emotions came out as anger, withdrawal, defensiveness, or silence.

I also noticed that many people cannot take accountability, admit fault, or say, "I am wrong" because they are rooted in shame.

No one had ever taught them how to communicate emotional needs.

Empathy is a skill.

Emotional expression is a skill.

Healthy communication is a skill.

Many individuals are taught conditional love, which is always based on performance. It is hard to be raised in homes based on conditional love. One must learn how to take accountability, understand shame, and know they are not always perfect. There is a lot of structure in the mind that needs to be redone, restructured, and reformed by family patterns.

I worked with many couples in which both partners were constantly offended by the other, yet neither could articulate what they needed. One wanted appreciation but expressed criticism. The other wanted respect but expressed distance. Both felt misunderstood. Both felt unloved.

However, despite the conflict, there was no disorder.

It was underdeveloped emotional language.

Children who are not allowed to cry often grow into adults who struggle to articulate grief. Children who were never comforted often grow into adults who struggle to comfort others. When emotional development is stunted early, relational breakdown later in life becomes far more likely.

What I observed repeatedly was not pathology, it was immaturity in emotional expression.

Research on childhood emotional neglect shows that when a child's emotions are ignored or dismissed, they often grow up with difficulty identifying their feelings, regulating their emotions, and forming healthy relationships. In some cases, these early wounds can contribute to narcissistic patterns later in life as individuals develop defensive identities to protect themselves from shame, insecurity, or unmet emotional needs. Studies have found that adverse childhood experiences and emotional neglect are associated with narcissistic traits, particularly forms of narcissism that are rooted in vulnerability, insecurity, and difficulty with emotional connection.

This does not mean every neglected child becomes narcissistic. Human development is complex. However, it does show that when children grow up without emotional validation, comfort, and guidance, their ability to form healthy relationships later in life can be deeply affected.

The skills required to build healthy relationships are rarely taught in school. They are rarely modeled consistently in homes.

However, we expect adults to navigate marriage, parenting, and conflict without ever having learned the basic language of feelings.

When I teach simple tools, such as how to name an emotion, state a need without accusation, and listen without defending, the atmosphere shifts.

Not because of a diagnosis.

But because of awareness.

This is one of the greatest deficits in our culture: we are not trained in emotional literacy.

When emotional illiteracy collides with stress, shame, trauma, or disappointment, the result looks like dysfunction.

However, often, it is simply an untrained relational capacity.

Over time, I witnessed that people who leaned into growth, whether through faith, accountability, discipline, or truth-telling, became more stable than those who avoided discomfort. There is a difference between numbing pain and maturing through it.

Some of the healthiest families I have encountered were not the richest. They were most connected through Christ, or the couple's parents were still together, and it seemed that, over generations, there were no divorces.

The Grandparents are involved with their grandchildren. There was discipline present throughout the couple's years of growing up. I also noticed there is open communication and acceptance.

Elders taught me patience. Many need socialization. When someone sat and listened to them, they came alive again. Serving the elderly is an honor. They do not need classification. They need companionship. Elders need to tell their story, their lives of the past and what they overcame, and I love hearing about their children, how they were successful in their jobs.

These are the best stories we can ever hear.

If there is one thing cleaning homes taught me, it is this:

Human beings are not primarily diagnostic problems.

They are relational beings.

Before I ever stepped into graduate school, before I ever read a diagnostic manual, I had already spent decades learning what loneliness looks like, what belonging heals, and what identity restores.

By the time I entered the clinical system, I believed it would strengthen what I already knew.

Instead, I discovered something else.

That is where the tension began.

CHAPTER 3

FROM GED TO GRADUATE SCHOOL

"**B**y the time I entered graduate school, I had already spent decades learning about people. What I did not yet understand was how differently the system would see them."

I failed school in the fifth grade. My parents kept signing me up for the next grade year after year, but I never saw the point of sitting in a classroom at such a young age. I did not fit the structure. I did not learn that way.

I remember sitting in class while other students earned good grades and made the honor roll, feeling completely lost. My parents came from a generation raised for the industrial workforce, not the academic system. School was something you endured, not something that shaped identity.

At the time, I assumed I would be pushed along from grade to grade. I did not feel that school defined me, but I began to believe I might not be academically intelligent. When a child feels lost in school long enough, they eventually stop believing the system was built for them.

Outside the classroom, however, I was alive. I met people, built friendships, and learned how to make money. That world made sense to me.

Years later, in my thirties, I decided to take the GED test. I bought a study book focused on the areas I needed to improve. When I passed, something shifted inside me.

I realized I was capable of learning.

I simply had not been ready for the system I had been placed in.

I discovered something important about myself: I was a self-learner.

I did not require a classroom to understand information. In many ways, a classroom environment distracted me more than it helped me. While others thrived in structured instruction, I found that I learned best by reading, researching, thinking deeply, and applying what I learned on my own.

Educational researchers often describe this type of person as a self-directed learner, someone who takes initiative in discovering knowledge rather than waiting for instruction. Some people need structured teaching environments, but others learn through curiosity and independent exploration.

At that time in my life, I was praying and asking God what my calling was.

One word came to me clearly: Counselor.

That was it.

I did not understand counseling as a medical profession. I did not understand diagnostic structures, billing systems, or clinical regulation. I was supposed to help people. As the word in the Bible says, Jesus was a Counselor.

So, I assumed college was the only path.

I did not research programs or compare educational routes. I thought I needed to attend a strong Christian college, at least what I believed at the time, and pursue the degree.

When I realized the educational path could take ten years, I decided this would be the first long-term goal I had ever committed to.

For someone who never liked school, it was a significant step. However, I told myself, *if God asked me to do this, I would do it.*

I began my college journey at Stark State, where I completed my associate's degree. It was not easy. I struggled through it, but that struggle strengthened my resilience and my determination to keep going.

By that time, I was a single mother raising three boys.

Despite the challenges, I continued my education and eventually earned a business degree from Malone University. From there, I pursued a degree in Clinical Mental Health.

Looking back, I still wonder how I managed it all.

I was cleaning homes for a living while raising my children, taking them with me to work, homeschooling them, and trying to build a future at the same time. Cleaning homes eventually allowed me to purchase my own house, but there were many moments when I feared losing everything or failing to reach my goals.

Through those difficult seasons, the people around me supported me, and my faith kept me moving forward.

I had no family support.

I kept pushing, determined to break cycles that had never been broken before.

Along the way, something remarkable happened. Many of the homes I cleaned belonged to retired teachers, and several of them became mentors to me. They encouraged my education, guided me through school, and believed in my ability to grow.

Their mentorship became part of the foundation that helped me continue forward.

There were early warning signs I ignored when I entered my Clinical Mental Health program. One professor once told me she would "have to tame me." At the time, I thought that was a compliment. Looking back, I realized something deeper.

My passion could not be tamed.

I was relational, expressive, and deeply invested in people. That kind of intensity does not always fit comfortably inside academic systems.

Another professor, who later left the college, quietly expressed concern about my well-being in that environment. At the time, I assumed something must be wrong with me.

Now I see it differently.

I carried empathy, relational instincts, and freedom shaped by community life. Those qualities do not easily compress into structured institutional systems.

I enjoyed my beginning college classes, writing, speech, and cultural studies. My business degree taught me discipline. It proved that I could commit to something difficult and see it through.

College taught me about structure, authority, and long-term commitment. I was able to attend many of my classes online, which gave me the freedom I needed to learn.

However, it did not teach me relationships.

When I entered the Clinical Mental Health program, I assumed faith and counseling would integrate naturally. Because the college was Christian, I believed the gospel would be central in the training.

I was wrong.

During online classes, I enthusiastically spoke about Jesus and what God was doing in my internship experiences. Eventually, I was placed on probation and told I could not impose my beliefs on others.

The ethical codes and regulations blindsided me.

I began to realize there were strict boundaries around spiritual integration.

The system was highly structured.

You must:

- Use DSM-5-TR diagnostic criteria.

- Document symptoms that meet diagnostic standards.

- Create treatment plans aligned with those diagnoses.

- Treatment must be evidence-based.

Diagnosis guides billing, medical necessity, risk management, legal documentation, and treatment selection.

It was a standardized framework.

By the time I fully entered the Clinical Mental Health program, what became clear was how regulated the system truly was. I am not naturally structured.

I do not rely on alarm clocks. I wake naturally. I never walked into sessions with rigid plans. I moved through conversations relatedly.

When I tried to structure sessions according to the program's expectations, my clients felt it.

It did not feel authentic.

It did not feel relational.

That created tension inside me.

Was I rebellious?

Was I resisting authority?

Was something wrong with me?

As I moved through the program, I had to ask harder questions. Was my resistance pride?

I knew I was deeply spiritual. I believed God had given me wisdom and insight into people. I did not live like the world, and I did not think like the world.

However, I examined my heart honestly.

I did not want it to be pride.

I did not want it to be a rebellion.

I wrestled with that tension constantly.

Was I immature?

Was I anti-system?

Or was something fundamentally misaligned?

When we are not where we are meant to be, resistance often appears long before understanding does.

I felt that resistance long before I understood why.

School sometimes felt like being confined by rules that restricted my natural relational instincts. For the first time in my life, I felt something I had never experienced before: institutional confinement.

At the same time, I had to admit something humbling.

Perhaps I underestimated clinical need.

Perhaps I did not fully understand the difference between community support and psychiatric intervention.

Perhaps I had romanticized relational care while overlooking real risk.

Then something became clear.

The system was not designed to form identity.

It was designed to manage risk.

That realization changed everything.

I had already established my identity long before entering the system. The clinical system was not there to shape identity. It existed to assess liability, reduce harm, and stabilize the crisis.

Once I understood that, some of my resistance softened.

Severe psychiatric crises require structure.

There is protection in boundaries.

There is wisdom in safeguards.

The system exists for a reason.

However, that reason is not identity formation.

What I wish I had known before entering the clinical mental health degree.

If I could speak to my younger self before enrolling, I would say:

- Counseling in this system means medical billing.

- Diagnosis is mandatory.

- Faith integration has defined limits.

- Empathy must follow structured protocols.

- Passion alone is not enough.

I asked myself constantly:

Did I misunderstand what "counselor" meant?

Was I called to a profession or to a purpose?

That question became the hardest of all.

A profession provides structure, recognition, and income.

Purpose sets the soul on fire.

Some people can hold their calling inside a system.

I am not wired that way.

I have always had an intense personality.

I do not function well in lukewarm environments.

During school, I often felt as though my relationship with God was being compartmentalized.

That unsettled me deeply.

Still, I do not see my education as punishment.

I see it as exposure.

It revealed something important.

There are two systems.

One manages risk.

One builds identity.

I was being trained to translate human lives into codes.

What I was experiencing personally had already been described in research.

Research in sociology and psychology has described a similar tension. Scholars have written about the medicalization of human struggles, in which personal, relational, or spiritual difficulties are categorized as medical conditions requiring diagnosis and documentation (Conrad, 2007).

In most clinical systems, insurance reimbursement requires a formal diagnostic code, which means counselors must translate complex human experiences into structured classifications.

Many clinicians report tension between the relational purpose that first drew them to the profession and the administrative requirements that structure modern mental health systems, including documentation, diagnostic labeling, and risk management (Maslach & Leiter, 2016).

What happens when human stories do not fit the codes designed to classify them? That tension followed me into the internship.

That is where everything intensified.

The classroom taught me the system.

However, internships would show me something far more complicated, with the mental health systems documentation requirements, diagnostic labeling, and risk management protocols (Maslach & Leiter, 2016)

What happens when human stories do not fit the codes designed to classify them?

PART II

WHEN STRUGGLE BECOMES DIAGNOSIS

CHAPTER 4

WHAT THE CLINICAL DEGREE ACTUALLY TEACHES

When I entered clinical mental health training, I was stepping into advanced relational work, helping people form identity, process childhood wounds, and build long-term resilience.

What I faced instead was a system structured primarily around regulated treatment, diagnosis, and risk management. I felt like when I went to the doctor's office, they typed all my symptoms in, and the computer came back with what it generated with medicine to prescribe.

In graduate school, we were taught:

- Theory & Techniques I & II

- Assessment models

- Addictions counseling frameworks

- Internship structure

- DSM-5-TR diagnostic criteria

- Treatment planning aligned with diagnosis

- Documentation standards

- Medical requirements

- Insurance billing compliance

Diagnosis is not optional.

Insurance reimbursement requires it.

Without a diagnosis:

- Services are not billable.

- Treatment is not considered medically necessary.

- Categorization is structurally tied to payment.

That reality deserves examination.

The Tension I Could Not Ignore.

I remember sitting in class feeling a tension I could not explain.

I was not opposed to theory.

I was not opposed to structure.

Nevertheless, I felt something deeper was missing.

I had already seen how identity forms in living rooms, kitchens, and communities.

What I was learning felt like management, not transformation.

That internal conflict stayed with me throughout my training. I often felt robotic and unable to express myself. I would sit in online classes thinking, *'This is not passion for people; this is labeling.'*

I was placed on probation several times because I openly talked about culture, and the professor believed others in the class were taking offense. I found that confusing. I believed discussing culture was exactly why we were in school.

Once again, I felt pressured to conform to the norm.

However, I had spent years inside homes with people from many cultural backgrounds, and not once did we take offense when discussing differences.

I began asking myself tough questions. They were telling me I was not culturally competent, but I had lived and worked among diverse families for decades. In reality, the professor seemed uncomfortable with open discussion. These people were blindly influenced by education rather than by interaction.

Increasingly, I felt pushed to conform to something that was not authentically me.

I also witnessed situations where counselors within the system formed inappropriate relationships with clients. I observed ethical boundaries blurred because conformity within the system was often prioritized over confronting uncomfortable realities.

The Structural Distinction

Theories such as Attachment Theory and Family Systems acknowledge childhood wounds, generational trauma, and relational identity formation.

I was not against those theories.

The tension was not about childhood.

The tension was about structure.

While the theories are relational, the system they operate requires:

- Diagnosis

- Impairment documentation

- Risk assessment

- Symptom measurement

- Billing justification

The DSM asks:

- What symptoms are present?

- How long have they lasted?

- How severe are they?

- How impairing are they?

It does not ask:

- What shaped this person's character?

- What identity are they forming?

- What role does belonging play in their healing?

- What meaning are they making from their struggle?

The DSM organizes suffering.

It does not form identity.

I began to realize something clearly.

The system was not designed to form identity.

It was designed to manage risk.

Risk management is necessary.

Risk management and identity formation are not the same thing.

That distinction changed everything for me.

At times, I struggled internally because I knew the Word of God and what it teaches about transformation and identity. Nevertheless, within the system, I was told we could not impose our beliefs on others.

Meanwhile, I had entered a Christian college believing that spiritual truth would be central to healing and restoration.

In my mind, it felt confusing. I believed people could experience freedom and salvation through the Word of God, yet the system placed strict boundaries around those conversations.

The Confusion Around Christian Counseling Programs

One of the questions that eventually forced me to stop and think was this: How can a college call a program *Christian counseling* if the ethical guidelines governing the profession require counselors to remain religiously neutral?

This is a question many Christian students begin asking once they enter graduate counseling programs.

Most licensed counseling programs, including those at Christian universities, must follow the same professional ethical standards required for licensure. These standards are set by organizations such as the American Counseling Association (ACA) and state licensing boards. The ethical codes emphasize client autonomy and prohibit counselors from imposing their personal values or religious beliefs on clients (American Counseling Association, 2014).

In practice, this means a counselor cannot openly teach or apply biblical truth unless the client specifically requests spiritual discussion. The counselor must remain neutral and cannot attempt to persuade the client toward their personal beliefs.

Because of these ethical requirements, many programs labeled "Christian counseling" still use the same diagnostic systems, clinical frameworks, and professional boundaries as secular counseling programs.

The curriculum typically includes psychological theory, the Diagnostic and Statistical Manual of Mental Disorders (DSM), and evidence-based clinical practices required for licensure.

Researchers studying Christian counseling education have acknowledged this tension. Christian counseling programs often seek to integrate theology with psychological science, but they must still operate within the ethical and regulatory frameworks governing the counseling profession (Tan, 2011).

For students entering these programs expecting counseling to resemble the biblical words of testimony and discipleship, the reality can be surprising.

Biblical counseling emphasizes spiritual authority, repentance, mentorship, and transformation through the Word of God. The model seen throughout Scripture involves believers speaking the truth, correcting one another in love, mentoring others, and helping them grow spiritually.

Clinical counseling, however, is structured around diagnosis, symptom management, and ethical neutrality.

These are two quite different frameworks.

This does not necessarily mean Christian colleges are intentionally deceiving students. In many cases, they are attempting to operate in both worlds, providing faith-based education while still meeting the professional requirements necessary for licensure.

The result can be confusing for students who expect a program called *Christian counseling* to function primarily from a biblical counseling model.

Greater transparency may be needed.

Students considering these programs deserve to understand the distinction clearly:

- Biblical counseling, which is rooted in discipleship and spiritual authority

- Clinical mental health counseling, which operates within professional psychological frameworks and ethical neutrality

Both may serve important roles, but they are not the same thing.

Understanding that distinction allows students to pursue the path that best aligns with their calling.

Incentives and Categorization

If payment requires a diagnosis, and treatment continuation requires documentation of impairment, then financial incentives can influence categorization.

This does not imply malicious intent.

It reflects structural design.

When reimbursement depends on diagnostic classification, and community-based mentorship is not billable, the system will naturally prioritize what can be reimbursed.

This raises important policy questions:

- Are clients fully informed when diagnoses are assigned for reimbursement?

- Do patients understand how their notes are documented and used?

- Are diagnostic continuation patterns independently reviewed?

- Does reimbursement structure unintentionally incentivize longer treatment duration?

- Are non-clinical community alternatives funded at comparable levels?

These are governance questions, not accusations.

Where My Conflict Deepened

Throughout my training, I felt a growing divide between what I had witnessed in real life and what I was being trained to document.

In homes and communities, I witnessed people change through truth, accountability, faith, and relationships.

In classrooms, I learned documentation, symptom clusters, and risk containment.

Both have purpose.

However, they are not interchangeable.

The deeper work I longed to do was identity transformation.

The system I was trained in prioritized liability and reimbursement structure.

That difference matters.

I could not build relationships with individuals the way I had in homes, offices, and communities. If I expressed my beliefs too strongly, it was considered unethical.

Slowly, I felt my natural gifts being constrained.

None of the clinical notes included Christianity or purpose. They were all symptom-based and treatment-centered.

There were moments when I even said I would lay down my license to save a soul and lead them to God, and that statement raised serious concerns within the program.

During those seasons, I prayed often, asking God where my true purpose was within all of this.

Putting God First in Counseling

At the center of this entire discussion is a truth that cannot be ignored. Human wisdom was never meant to replace God's wisdom. Throughout Scripture, guidance and counsel begin with one foundation: God first.

Proverbs teach:

"Trust in the Lord with all thine heart; and lean not unto thine own understanding. In all thy ways acknowledge him, and he shall direct thy paths." (Proverbs 3:5–6)

The Bible does not present human guidance as independent from God. Instead, wisdom, counsel, and direction flow from a relationship with Him.

The book of Proverbs repeatedly emphasizes that true wisdom begins with reverence for God:

"The fear of the Lord is the beginning of wisdom." (Proverbs 9:10)

In this model, counsel is not simply advice or emotional support. Counsel is guidance that aligns a person with truth, wisdom, and God's design for life.

This understanding shaped how communities historically approached guidance and mentorship. Elders, parents, pastors, and wise individuals provided counsel rooted in spiritual conviction, moral responsibility, and lived experience.

However, as modern psychological systems developed during the twentieth century, the foundation of counseling began to shift. Counseling increasingly became structured around scientific frameworks that prioritized human reasoning, diagnosis, and treatment models.

Spiritual authority was often removed in order to maintain professional neutrality.

Scholars describe this shift as part of a broader cultural movement toward the medicalization and professionalization of human struggles, in which problems once addressed through community, faith, and mentorship were interpreted through clinical and psychological systems (Conrad, 2007).

This does not mean clinical care has no place. Severe mental illness requires trained professionals and medical stabilization.

However, when spiritual wisdom is completely removed from guidance and identity formation, something essential is lost.

Humans were not created to rely on human systems alone.

We were created for a relationship with God.

We were created with identity.

We were created with purpose.

When God is placed first, wisdom, identity, and direction begin to take shape in a way that no system alone can provide.

Counsel that ignores this foundation may treat symptoms, but it cannot lead the soul. Restoring healthy communities requires a return to where wisdom begins.

It begins with God.

Transparency for Patients

One concern that emerged during my experience in the clinical system involved transparency with patients. In many cases, individuals were scheduled for what was described as a "two-hour assessment." However, they were not always clearly informed that the purpose of this process was to evaluate them for a clinical diagnosis.

This created tension for me because it sometimes felt as though vital information was not fully explained.

Research in medical ethics emphasizes that informed consent requires patients to understand the nature and purpose of evaluations, diagnoses, and treatment processes (American Medical Association, 2023). Transparency allows individuals to make informed decisions about their care and strengthens trust between patients and providers.

Patients deserve clarity about what is happening in the clinical process.

They should understand:

- When they are being evaluated for a diagnosis.

- How a diagnosis may affect insurance reimbursement.

- What documentation and clinical classification are required for billing?

- the difference between treatment for psychiatric impairment and relational or community support.

Ethicists emphasize that informed consent should not only address treatment risks but also provide clear communication about how healthcare systems operate, including diagnostic classification and reimbursement structures (Beauchamp & Childress, 2019).

Trust grows when patients understand the systems guiding their care. Transparency strengthens autonomy, protects patient rights, and helps individuals make decisions that align with their needs.

Accountability Oversight

Licensed clinicians operate under ethical codes and state regulations.

Oversight exists.

However, oversight must evolve alongside reimbursement design.

Policy reform should consider:

- Independent review of diagnostic continuation patterns.

- Clear audit standards focused on clinical necessity and integrity.

- Strengthened accountability structures tied to billing.

- Clearer distinctions between clinical impairment and community-based support.

Accountability protects patients.

It protects ethical clinicians.

It protects the integrity of the profession.

Educational Responsibility

Graduate programs must clearly inform students that clinical counseling operates within:

- Insurance reimbursement models

- •Medical standards

- Risk management frameworks

- Liability structures

Students should understand the distinction between:

Clinical Treatment

Community Mentorship

Pastoral Counseling

Identity Formation

These are different models with different purposes.

Blurring them creates confusion for both practitioners and the public.

Clarifying Realization

I respect clinical care.

I respect licensing.

I respect the necessity of risk management.

However, identity formation and reimbursement structures are not the same thing.

If reimbursement drives categorization, reform must ensure categorization remains clinically necessary rather than structurally incentivized.

Clinical care stabilizes impairment.

Community builds resilience.

Both are necessary.

However, they must be clearly distinguished.

What I had learned in the classroom was structure.

What I had lived in homes and communities was relationships.

An internship would be the place where those two worlds collided.

That conflict forced me to face a question I could no longer ignore:

Was I being trained to help people or to manage their symptoms?

I wondered how I came to be a counselor, the only one I knew, and the term counselor was in the Bible. The only structure I knew was in the Bible. As I began searching, I came across evidence that supported my feelings.

How Counseling Moved from Churches to Psychology

For most of history, counseling was not a medical profession. Families, elders, and religious groups provided guidance and support.

In Christian communities, spiritual guidance often occurred through pastoral care, discipleship, and mentorship within the church. Pastors and elders provided counsel based on Scripture, prayer, wisdom, and lived experience. The goal was not diagnosis, but spiritual formation, moral guidance, and restoration.

During the late nineteenth and early twentieth centuries, a major shift began. As modern psychology developed as a scientific discipline, emotional struggles and behavioral problems increasingly came to be interpreted through psychological and medical frameworks rather than spiritual or moral ones.

By the mid-twentieth century, professional psychology and psychiatry had begun to replace many of the counseling roles previously held within churches and communities. Experts in sociology and history refer to this shift as the psychologization of human problems. Issues formerly resolved through moral advice, mentorship, or spiritual guidance are now often seen as psychological disorders that need treatment from professionals (Conrad, 2007).

At the same time, counseling gradually became a licensed profession governed by regulatory boards, ethical codes, and diagnostic systems such as the Diagnostic and Statistical Manual of Mental Disorders (DSM). These frameworks require counselors to operate within structured professional guidelines designed to ensure neutrality and protect client autonomy.

Because of these professional requirements, modern clinical counseling developed as a religiously neutral field. Counselors are trained to respect clients' beliefs without imposing their own values or spiritual perspectives.

As a result, the modern counseling profession and the biblical model of discipleship developed along different paths.

Biblical counseling focuses on spiritual authority, repentance, mentorship, and transformation through truth.

Clinical counseling focuses on diagnosis, symptom management, and therapeutic neutrality.

Many Christian universities today attempt to integrate these two models. However, because counseling programs must still meet licensing requirements and professional ethical standards, they often operate within the same clinical framework used in secular counseling education.

This historical shift helps explain why students entering "Christian counseling" programs sometimes experience tension between their faith convictions and the professional structure of the counseling field.

The problem is not always that faith is dismissed. Rather, the professional system governing counseling was built on a different foundation.

Understanding this history helps clarify an important distinction:

Biblical discipleship and clinical counseling may both seek to help people, but they operate from different assumptions about authority, truth, and the role of spiritual guidance.

Recognizing that distinction allows individuals to pursue the path that aligns with their calling.

CHAPTER 5

WHEN DIAGNOSES BECOMES A DEFAULT

Over time, I began noticing a pattern. People rarely ask questions about the process they enter.

They do not ask:

How are you analyzing me during these sessions?

What kind of notes are you taking?

What evidence is this based on?

What exactly have you diagnosed me with?

Many people simply go with the flow.

They take the first appointment available.

They trust the process without asking questions.

Convenience often replaces curiosity.

Very few pauses to ask whether other options exist.

Most people trust the system. They assume that because a clinician went to college, the process must automatically be correct.

Many also do not realize how the system functions. Frequently, after a counselor provides a diagnosis, much of the ongoing interaction with the client is managed by caseworkers, who typically receive considerably lower pay. The relationship that initially begins with a counselor often changes quickly.

For many clients, this meant instability.

One of the most common complaints I heard was that they had seen many different counselors. They would finally begin to build trust, complete the intake assessment, and then the counselor would change.

Relationships were replaced with turnover.

Diagnosis was no longer simply a clinical tool.

It had become the entry point into the entire system.

Many clients never fully realized they were being diagnosed at all.

Marriage counseling provides one example. Couples often enter therapy because they are experiencing relational conflict. However, for insurance billing purposes, individual diagnoses are frequently required. Even when the core issue is relational, both must meet diagnostic criteria. I realized I was not the only one concerned about the diagnosis.

Concerns about diagnostic transparency are not new.

In a famous study, psychologist David Rosenhan sent healthy individuals into psychiatric hospitals claiming to hear a single voice. Once admitted, they behaved normally, yet staff interpreted their ordinary behavior as symptoms of mental illness. The study revealed how powerful diagnostic labels can become once assigned, sparking a major debate about the reliability of psychiatric classification (Rosenhan, 1973).

This research highlights why transparency, informed consent, and clear communication about diagnostic processes remain essential in mental health care. I remember sitting in supervision when statements were made that reflected how easily broad diagnostic categories could be applied.

That moment stayed with me.

It was not that the diagnosis was unnecessary.

It was how quickly it became automatic.

I often wished there were space to say to a client:

"Maybe what you need is mentorship, community guidance, or relational support rather than diagnosis."

Instead, diagnosis became the pathway that allowed services to continue.

This created an ethical tension for me.

I began to wonder what it would look like if a counselor could remain beside someone as a relational mentor without needing to translate every struggle into clinical language.

At the same time, I began to notice something else.

Many of the individuals entering the system were not coming in calmly.

They were coming in the middle of grief.

In the middle of a relational breakdown.

In the middle of an emotional crisis.

Yet even in those moments, they were often placed into a process that required waiting, assessment, and scheduling before meaningful support could begin.

Some were told to wait days.

Others were told to wait weeks.

By the time help became available, the moment that had brought them in had already shifted.

Sometimes, something has already been lost.

The Importance of Being There in the Moment

Through experience, I noticed something that I could not ignore.

The most valuable time to be present for someone is not weeks later.

It is in the middle of their need.

It is when a relationship breaks down.

When a child is struggling.

When a family is in conflict

When someone is overwhelmed at work.

Those are the moments when people are most open, most vulnerable, and most capable of change.

In those moments, people often turn to pastoral counselors, mentors, or trusted relationships. They are not always looking for a diagnosis. They are looking for guidance, stability, and someone who will sit with them until they can regain a sense of clarity and resilience.

Over time, I became intentional about remaining available.

If someone was going through a breakup, I stayed present as they processed the grief, even when it lasted for months. I learned that access mattered. Growth did not happen on schedule. It happened in moments.

I had people call me in the middle of a crisis, telling me they had to wait three weeks for an appointment with a mental health counselor. Meanwhile, they were experiencing emotional breakdowns, overwhelming thoughts, or relational collapse.

I chose to keep my line open.

I never had someone take advantage of that because I remained professional.

What I noticed was this: by the time many people reached their next scheduled appointment, the moment for growth had already passed. Sometimes something harmful has already happened. The window where reflection, awareness, and change were possible had closed.

I would even allow teenagers to call when they needed someone to talk to. It was important that they didn't suppress what they were feeling or what they were experiencing at that moment, because they often wouldn't return to it later.

When the time came for their appointment, they often didn't show up.

Availability mattered.

What I learned through experience is now supported by research.

Studies on crisis intervention consistently show that timely, immediate support improves outcomes. When individuals receive help in the moment of distress, they are more likely to stabilize emotionally and move toward resolution.

Crisis line research has shown that most individuals experience a reduction in distress during the interaction itself. In many cases, the conversation in the moment provides relief before any long-term treatment begins.

Crisis intervention models are built on this principle. They are designed for immediate stabilization, emotional support, and helping individuals return to a functional state as quickly as possible.

However, there remains a gap.

Many individuals are still asked to wait days or weeks for scheduled appointments while they are in the middle of emotional or psychological distress.

That delay matters.

Because the moment when someone is most open to reflection, most aware of their pain, and most willing to change is often temporary.

When support is delayed, that moment can pass.

This does not mean clinical care is unnecessary.

Severe psychiatric conditions require structured treatment, stabilization, and professional oversight.

However, not every moment of distress is a clinical disorder.

Some moments are opportunities.

Opportunities for awareness.

Opportunities for growth.

Opportunities for change.

When someone is met with presence, guidance, and connection at that moment, the outcome can be quite different.

The difference is not always in the treatment.

Sometimes, the difference is simply a matter of timing.

The Structure Behind the Default

Modern clinical mental health care operates within insurance-based systems.

Insurance companies require:

- A DSM diagnosis

- Documentation of impairment

- Evidence of medical necessity

Without diagnosis:

- Services are not reimbursed

- Treatment cannot be billed

When payment requires a diagnosis, diagnosis becomes the gateway to access.

The first session becomes less about:

"Tell me your story."

More about: "What criteria do you meet?"

For many clients, the system feels convenient. Medicaid often fully covers services. For others with private insurance, the first sessions may be free or require only a small co-pay. College students often seek therapy simply because it is covered by insurance for a certain number of visits, then they drop it.

However, this structure creates unintended consequences.

When services are free or easily accessible, some individuals treat the system casually. Sessions become more like social visits than intentional treatment. Others move through multiple counselors over time, accumulating different diagnoses along the way.

Paperwork rarely follows them clearly from one provider to another.

Ironically, greater transparency and consistency in records could increase accountability and self-awareness for everyone involved.

Another pattern I encountered involved requests for diagnoses of emotional support animals. Many people needed a diagnosis to keep an animal in their housing environment. Others needed diagnoses to qualify for benefits or maintain Social Security eligibility.

In training, we were often told, "We are not investigators. We give the client what they request." These experiences revealed how strongly diagnosis functions as a gatekeeper within multiple systems.

Short Term Treatment, Long Term Cycles

Short-term interventions are commonly used in the design of treatment plans. Six to eight weeks is common.

However, reassessments frequently occur for continued billing cycles. Documentation must demonstrate ongoing impairment to justify reimbursement.

This creates a difficult structural question:

If improvement reduces billability, what incentives support discharge?

This question is not about accusing individual clinicians.

It is about examining incentive alignment within the system.

Expansion Into Public Systems

Diagnosis also intersects with broader public systems.

In certain contexts, a diagnosis may be required for:

- Disability support

- Housing accommodations

- Service animals

- Educational accommodations

- Social Security eligibility

When access to resources depends on diagnosis, categorization becomes powerful.

The mental health system serves as a gateway to public benefit systems. That level of authority deserves transparency and accountability.

Cultural Medicalization

The shift toward clinical interpretation did not happen overnight. Over time, modern culture has increasingly interpreted human struggles through medical language.

Grief can quickly become depression.

Research shows that grief is a natural human response to loss, even though the boundary between grief and clinical depression has become widely debated. Earlier psychiatric guidelines included a "bereavement exclusion," recognizing that intense sadness following the death of a loved one should not automatically be diagnosed as major depressive disorder. The removal of this exclusion raised concerns among researchers that normal grief reactions could be misclassified as clinical depression (Bonanno, 2004; Wakefield & First, 2012).

Shyness can become social anxiety.

Fear and anxiety are normal human responses that help individuals navigate uncertainty and new environments. Nevertheless, diagnostic expansion has raised concerns that everyday emotional experiences may sometimes be classified as clinical disorders when diagnostic thresholds are applied too broadly (Frances, 2013; Stein & Stein, 2008).

Marital conflict can become a mood disorder.

Research in relationship psychology shows that ongoing hostile conflict can contribute to emotional distress. However, disagreement itself is a normal part of relationships and can become an opportunity for growth when couples develop communication and conflict resolution skills (Whisman & Beach, 2001; Gottman & Levenson, 1992).

Some cases truly require clinical care.

Not every human struggle is a psychiatric impairment.

Medical language carries authority.

It reduces ambiguity.

It provides access.

It can also reshape how people see themselves.

When Identity Becomes Diagnoses

When diagnosis becomes the primary lens, identity can become secondary.

Childhood energy can become ADHD.

I have known individuals who, once given a label, could not move past it. The diagnosis became comfortable even when they desired change.

Parents often say immediately:

"My son has ADHD."

I sometimes respond:

"That may also mean he carries traits suited for a powerful purpose."

Some researchers have suggested that traits associated with ADHD, such as heightened alertness, novelty-seeking, and rapid responses to changing conditions, may have been advantageous in earlier human environments.

Research examining a dopamine receptor gene variant associated with ADHD traits found that individuals carrying this variant showed better health outcomes in nomadic populations compared to settled populations (Eisenberg et al., 2008).

This perspective does not claim ADHD is simply an advantage.

However, it highlights an important principle:

Human behavior develops within environments.

Traits that appear dysfunctional in rigid institutional systems may have served meaningful roles in other contexts.

I know this personally.

Even at fifty years old, I must run for fifty minutes a day and swim for forty minutes at night. My energy remains high.

Imagine that energy when I was a child.

I ran down the streets.

I rode horses.

I rarely become tired.

Today, I am an entrepreneur and an evangelist by nature.

Traits that once looked like "too much energy" became part of my purpose.

The Deeper Concern

My concern was that clinical care should never disappear.

My concern was that it was becoming everything.

When community structures weaken,

When churches disengage,

When families fracture,

When mentorship declines,

Clinical systems absorb what the community once held.

However, clinical systems are not intended to establish identity.

They are designed to manage risk.

Why Therapy and Church Remain Separate

Historically, the care of the soul was rooted within the authority of Scripture and the life of the church.

The Bible presents healing, wisdom, correction, and restoration as functions of spiritual community, mentorship, and obedience to God's Word.

Modern psychotherapy developed later within secular academic and medical institutions. As psychology emerged as a scientific discipline, it was intentionally structured apart from religious authority, operating within a religiously neutral framework.

Because therapists collaborate with people from many belief systems, professional ethics require them to avoid presenting religious doctrine as authority.

For this reason, therapy and the church operate in different domains. Clinical counseling addresses psychological distress within a secular medical structure.

The church operates under the authority of Scripture, guiding spiritual formation, character development, and identity.

Scripture describes this authority clearly:

2 Timothy 3:16–17 "All Scripture is breathed out by God and profitable for teaching, for reproof, for correction, and for training in righteousness."

Furthermore, healing within the community is emphasized:

James 5:16 "Confess your sins to one another and pray for one another, that you may be healed."

Clinical systems address certain needs.

However, spiritual authority belongs to the Word of God.

The Reform Question

Diagnosis becomes the default when:

- Reimbursement requires it

- Risk culture depends on it

- Education trains reflexively toward it

- Public benefits rely on it

- Community alternatives lack funding

The issue is not individual greed.

It is a structural concentration of authority.

If a diagnosis opens every door, it will be widely used.

Reform must focus on:

- Transparency for patients

- Independent review of billing patterns

- Clear distinctions between impairment and relational distress

- Funding for community-based support

- Accountability protections for trainees

Clinical care is necessary.

However, when every human struggle is filtered through diagnosis, the system begins carrying responsibilities it was never designed to hold.

That is not a character failure.

It is a systems problem.

Diagnosis can describe symptoms.

It can organize treatment.

No diagnosis should ever define a human being.

Before anyone is diagnosed

Before anyone is a case file

Before anyone is a code

They are a person.

A person was never meant to be reduced to a number.

You are not a code

CHAPTER 6

INTERSHIP REALITY. WHEN SYSTEMS BECOME REALITY

Over the years, I noticed another pattern among the individuals who came through my office. Some of them had been involved with the system since childhood. Many had experienced severe trauma early in life, abuse, abandonment, or instability in adoptive homes that were not prepared to care for the wounds those children carried.

As they grew older, their symptoms were eventually labeled under diagnoses such as PTSD.

By the time they reached adulthood, many were receiving Social Security support and living in facilities connected to the system. The diagnosis followed them into adulthood, and with it came a stigma that shaped how others saw them and often how they saw themselves.

Many of these individuals struggled to hold jobs. Something as simple as a supervisor speaking to them in a firm tone could trigger a strong reaction rooted in earlier experiences of rejection or authority abuse. Their responses were often misunderstood by employers who did not know the history behind those reactions.

Over time, I realized that many of these individuals had been repeatedly rejected throughout their lives. Parents had rejected them, sometimes rejected by adoptive families, and later rejected by society when they struggled to function in environments that expected stability they had never been taught. Eventually, many learned to survive within the system itself.

When someone grows up receiving benefits, housing support, and structured assistance, it can become difficult to leave that environment. In many ways, it functions similarly to long-term welfare dependency. If obtaining a job means losing food assistance, housing support, or medical coverage, the system can unintentionally discourage independence.

In some other countries, when individuals begin working, they continue receiving food and medical support for a period while they transition into stability. That kind of gradual transition allows people to build independence without the fear of losing everything at once.

What I noticed was that many of the individuals I worked with were capable of growth when they were supported, rather than only through administrative support.

Some had never learned basic life skills that many people take for granted. I helped some of them learn how to drive because they had spent their entire lives relying on buses and transportation programs. As they gained confidence and built relationships in the community, they began experiencing small but critical changes.

However, something else became clear.

Even as individuals began to improve, their minds often struggled to let go of what was familiar. The system had become the structure of their life.

This showed me something important.

A diagnosis such as PTSD may describe real trauma, but trauma does not have to define a person forever. Human beings have the capacity to heal, grow stronger, and develop resilience through relationships, mentorship, and meaningful life experiences.

Rejection can become a wound.

It can also become a source of strength when individuals learn how to persevere through it.

Many of the individuals I encountered needed more than treatment plans.

They needed mentors.

They needed community.

They needed relationships.

They needed someone to help them build life skills and a sense of identity.

Institutional environments often began early in their lives, and over time, the damage of institutionalization itself became part of the challenge.

Some individuals attempted to come off medication but struggled because their bodies had adjusted to those medications over prolonged periods of time. Their brains had adapted to the chemical support they were receiving. This added another layer of complexity, making independence even harder.

I have also supported college students who, as children, were placed in several different environments, including foster homes, orphanages, and adoptive families that eventually relinquished care. Many of them arrived in adulthood heavily medicated and deeply isolated.

Some struggled with self-harm because they wanted to feel something again after years of emotional numbness.

These young adults often missed developmental stages that most children experience earlier in life. When they finally entered environments where they felt safe enough to explore identity, they sometimes went through those stages during their college years rather than during childhood.

However, a remarkable change occurred when they were treated as individuals rather than merely as their diagnoses.

When I focused on their identity, their purpose, and their potential rather than only their symptoms, many of them began to flourish.

They started making friends in the community.

They bought cars.

They adopted pets.

They began building lives.

They slowly stepped out of isolation and fear.

Watching those transformations reinforced something I had begun realizing for years. Human beings do not flourish through classification alone.

They flourish through relationships.

Professional Environments and the Language of Diagnosis

Later, when I worked in professional office environments, I began noticing another pattern.

Many of these organizations employed individuals with advanced education. On the surface, everything appeared organized and professional. Policies were followed. Titles were respected. Professional language was used.

Something else was happening beneath the surface.

Conversations are increasingly centered around diagnoses, labels, and categories. People sometimes describe themselves and others in clinical terms rather than in terms of character, responsibility, or growth.

I began noticing a shift.

Instead of asking how people could grow stronger through difficulty, the question often became which diagnosis explained the difficulty.

Instead of strengthening communication between coworkers, relationships sometimes became filtered through labels.

Instead of focusing on the work itself and the relationships within the workplace, attention often shifted toward personal classifications.

What struck me most was that the very environments designed to help people were often struggling with the same relational breakdowns they were attempting to treat.

Offices still experienced gossip.

Coworkers still struggled with communication.

Professional environments still carry misunderstandings, conflicts, and isolation.

Systems could organize information.

However, they could not replace the work required to build healthy relationships.

That realization stayed with me.

Human beings are not primarily problems to be categorized.

They are people learning how to grow, work, communicate, and belong.

Growth can be uncomfortable.

It can be painful.

Nevertheless, it is also how resilience is built and how individuals reach important milestones in life.

In some workplaces, I even found myself teaching supervisors how to communicate more effectively with their employees, regulate their emotions, and speak in ways that build teams rather than divisions.

Sometimes the problem was not a diagnosis.

Sometimes the problem was simply that people had never been taught how to relate well to one another.

When we fail to distinguish between normal human development and mental illness, we risk interfering with the natural process of maturity.

When maturity is delayed or avoided, the consequences often appear later in life.

Systems can provide support.

However, they were never designed to replace the human relationships that teach us how to grow.

The Internship Turning Point

I worked in a school building as an intern.

My supervisor handed me marketing pamphlets and told me I could "sell diagnoses" to students.

Soon, kids lined up at my door.

My caseload exploded.

Money flowed in.

I felt dishonest.

Most of those children did not have diagnosable disorders.

They wanted:

- Someone to listen to

- Relationship

- Identity

- Direction

I gathered these children in my room for lunch and had them write letters to their teachers about what they did not like. I taught them communication skills and identity formation. Eventually, the parents came to see me and witnessed the changes.

I went into these children's homes and taught parents how to build relationships with their children instead of repeating patterns of abuse. I would drive around with the kids, listen to music, and spend time with them one-on-one. That quality time meant the world to them.

They began opening up about what was happening in their homes.

They began trusting me.

I recall certain African American students who thought their race prevented them from achieving anything in life. That mindset was painful to see. I worked to help them rebuild identity and purpose.

Students who had stolen things would return them. They began taking accountability. I allowed them to dance, listen to music, and build relationships with each other, rather than cause chaos.

I formed rapport quickly.

I spoke truth in love.

I focused on identity, not symptom checklists.

Later, I interned with adults at a large organization and quickly learned that most of the issues people faced were relational.

Out of seventy-five clients, only a small number required intensive DSM-level clinical intervention.

I grew quickly in that environment. Most people did not need long-term therapy. After a while, they simply wanted someone to talk to.

People were transitioning into careers, searching for jobs, navigating relationships, and learning to compromise. Many were young adults struggling with identity, purpose, and direction.

Eventually, I was accused of emotional manipulation.

I was told I did not align with the diagnostic model.

That is when something becomes clear.

When relational authenticity clashes with a medical billing structure, conflict emerges

PART III

DRAWING THE BOUNDARY

CHAPTER 7

TREATMENT VS TRANSFORMATION

I have sat with individuals who were terrified of their own bodies. Racing heart. Sweaty palms. Fear of losing control. Fear of dying. Panic attacks are real. They are not imaginary.

The treatment model is valuable here.

- Diagnosis

- Grounding skills

- Breathing techniques

- Sometimes medication

The goal is stabilization and reduction of episodes.

That matters.

What I noticed is that panic often sits on top of something deeper, fear of rejection, fear of failure, fear rooted in childhood abandonment, or fear intertwined through trauma.

Fear of the worst-case scenario happening.

For instance, when someone abandons us, gets up, and leaves a relationship with no reconciliation or explanation, this is abandonment. Now we feel we cannot live without them. Somewhere in the past, we might have been abandoned in our lives, which, over time, causes even bigger PTSD.

My whole life, I was the one who abandoned people with no thought of the consequences. Looking back now, I asked my ex how he could tolerate me leaving him so many times, and didn't it hurt him?

As I got older, I finally faced a person who had abandoned me after three months of marriage. I could not breathe. I was traumatized by how someone could leave with no heart, no feeling, and their mind switched double-minded so suddenly, never to come back.

I had breathing attacks at night so badly, and eventually, I did start dating two years after that, only to go through the abandonment cycle all over again.

My responses got worse. I was screaming, yelling, and trying to hold on to something that did not see my value.

After five years of this continued cycle, I became immune to it. I understood it is not me; it is their self-centeredness that cannot cope and seek control through abandonment.

I built resilience, and it is okay if someone leaves.

The amazing thing God showed me is that I am complete and whole, but it was the process of learning my identity and purpose, and that, with or without someone, I am complete.

No treatment could have helped me relieve symptoms and helped me ground my mindset during the process.

However, it was the process of facing continued abandonment that built my perseverance and awareness of self-love.

At a certain point, one outgrows these types of people and realizes there was something incomplete about themselves that made them feel the need to fix others.

Treatment reduces episodes.

Resilience change's identity.

Resilience asks:

What am I afraid of?

What belief is underneath this panic?

Who am I if I can face this and survive it?

Gradual exposure builds strength.

Emotional regulation builds tolerance.

Supportive relationships reduce isolation.

Identity reframing shifts from:

"I am anxious."

to

"I am capable of facing fear."

Treatment helps someone survive the storm.

Resilience helps them walk back into it without collapsing.

I met a man who had panic attacks so severe that he was in a relationship with a therapist. Every time they got into a fight, he would not leave. Instead, it caused even more abuse because in his mind, he thought that if he left, he would never see her again.

The police would get involved, setting off a major cycle of chaos that would repeat every few days.

These cycles are hard to break.

They cause consequences because it is hard to release without panic.

It is hard to stay vulnerable and say:

"Ok, I can live without them."

"I do not deserve this treatment."

"This is not healthy, how I am acting."

Treatment Model

- Diagnose Panic Disorder

- Teaching grounding techniques

- Possibly prescribe medication

- Reduce frequency and intensity

Goal: Stabilize symptoms.

Resilience Model

- Explore fear triggers

- Build confidence through gradual exposure

- Strengthen emotional regulation

- Develop supportive relationships

- Reframe identity from "I am anxious" to "I can face fear."

Goal: Increase long-term capacity and internal strength.

Treatment reduces episodes.

Resilience change's identity.

Research on Panic

Panic attacks are often treated exclusively as a clinical disorder, yet the physiological response underlying panic is rooted in normal human survival mechanisms.

Neuroscience research shows that the body's fear system, commonly known as the fight-or-flight response, is designed to activate in response to perceived threats, increasing heart rate, breathing, and alertness to prepare the body for danger (Cannon, 1932; LeDoux, 1996).

In many cases, panic attacks occur when these normal bodily sensations are misinterpreted as catastrophic, triggering escalating fear responses even in the absence of real danger (Clark, 1986; Clark & Beck, 2010).

Because of this, some researchers emphasize approaches that strengthen resilience rather than focusing only on symptom suppression. Gradual exposure to feared sensations and situations has been shown to help individuals build tolerance, reduce fear sensitivity, and regain confidence in their ability to regulate emotional responses (Foa & Kozak, 1986; Craske et al., 2014).

Social support and relational stability also play a significant role in regulating stress responses, as human nervous systems are strongly influenced by interpersonal connections (Coan, 2010; Siegel, 2012).

These findings suggest an important distinction:

The biological mechanisms behind panic are not inherently pathological. They are part of the normal human design for responding to a threat.

The challenge arises when these systems become hypersensitive or misinterpreted.

Effective care, therefore, requires more than simply reducing symptoms. It involves building emotional capacity, strengthening supportive relationships, and helping individuals develop confidence in their ability to face fear.

In this sense, resilience-based approaches aim not only to stabilize distress but to restore long-term psychological strength and adaptive functioning.

We want to get people out of survival mode into resilience.

Marital Conflict

This is one of the areas where I feel the strongest tension. I have already covered the research in the last chapter, but I will quickly summarize it here.

Many couples entering therapy do not realize that individual diagnoses will be assigned for insurance billing purposes, even when the primary issue is relational conflict rather than a psychiatric disorder.

Disagreement, emotional immaturity, and communication breakdown are familiar challenges in long-term relationships. Research in relationship psychology shows that conflict itself is not abnormal; in fact, the way couples manage disagreement is one of the strongest predictors of long-term relationship stability (Gottman & Levenson, 1992; Gottman, 1999).

Many couples struggle not because they have a mental illness, but because they were never taught emotional expression, conflict tolerance, or accountability within relationships. Family-of-origin patterns, early unmet emotional needs, and learned communication styles often shape how individuals respond to disagreement in adulthood (Bowen, 1978; Johnson, 2004).

For many couples, healing involves learning skills that were never modeled, such as communicating honestly, regulating emotional reactions, and staying connected during conflict. These are relational developmental skills, not necessarily psychiatric symptoms.

This does not automatically mean mental illness.

It often means growth is required.

I have seen couples who believed something was deeply wrong with them, only to discover they needed communication skills, accountability, and community support. When couples are surrounded by other couples who have endured similar seasons, shame tends to decrease. Perspective broadens. Identity as a team strengthens.

The most successful couples were those who took accountability, had self-awareness, and empathy. It is much harder when the relationship becomes one-sided, and neither partner holds these values.

Treatment Model

- Diagnose Adjustment Disorder or Anxiety (if criteria are met)

- Teach communication techniques

- Document symptom relief

- Reduce distress

Goal: Manage relational stress.

Resilience Model

- Teach emotional vocabulary

- Address family-of-origin dynamics

- Build accountability

- Strengthen shared purpose

- Develop conflict tolerance

Goal: Deepen maturity and commitment.

Treatment manages conflict.

Resilience strengthens the foundation of the relationship.

Teen Identity Crises

Many of the teenagers I sat with did not primarily want medication. They wanted to be heard.

They were searching for guidance, help in understanding their lives and their purpose. More than anything, they needed the language to express what they were experiencing.

Many were navigating divorce, fractured family systems, or feeling invisible in their own homes. Some displayed mood symptoms. Some met the criteria for clinical care. Others were navigating normal identity development without guidance.

Teenagers need language for their emotions.

They need structure and accountability.

They need to feel known.

In my experience, community support, mentors, strong family communication, and value formation often stabilized teens more effectively than symptom labeling alone.

Treatment Model

- Diagnosing Anxiety or Mood Disorder (if criteria are met)

- Provide coping skills

- Document symptom reduction

Goal: Reduce distress.

Resilience Model

- Teach emotional expression

- Strengthen family communication

- Develop purpose

- Build healthy peer support

Goal: Strengthen identity formation.

Treatment addresses distress.

Resilience shapes character.

Adolescence is a period of rapid psychological, emotional, and neurological development. Developmental research consistently shows that teenagers naturally experience heightened emotional intensity, identity questioning, and shifts in social belonging as they move toward adulthood.

Psychologist Erik Erikson described this stage as "identity versus role confusion," in which adolescents explore values, relationships, and purpose to form a stable sense of self (Erikson, 1968). During this period, mood fluctuations, emotional sensitivity, and experimentation with identity are common and often reflect normal developmental processes rather than psychiatric impairment.

Neuroscience research further explains that the adolescent brain is still developing, particularly in regions responsible for emotional regulation and decision-making. The prefrontal cortex, which governs impulse control and long-term planning, continues maturing into the mid-twenties, while emotional centers such as the amygdala are highly active during adolescence (Steinberg, 2014; Casey, Jones, & Hare, 2008).

This developmental imbalance helps explain why teenagers may experience strong emotions while still learning how to regulate them.

Social and relational environments also play a significant role in adolescent development. Research shows that supportive relationships with parents, mentors, and trusted adults significantly improve emotional resilience and reduce risk behaviors (Resnick et al., 1997; Scales & Leffert, 2004).

Adolescents who feel known, valued, and guided within families and communities are more likely to develop stable identity, emotional competence, and long-term well-being.

These findings suggest that while some adolescents may require clinical care for significant mental health conditions, many teens are navigating a normal developmental process that involves searching for meaning, belonging, and identity.

Effective support often includes helping adolescents develop emotional vocabulary, strengthening family communication, and providing mentorship and positive peer connections.

In this sense, addressing distress is important, but the deeper developmental task of adolescence is identity formation, learning who they are, what they value, and where they belong.

Adolescent Experimentation and Development

From my experience in various homes and workplaces, I am less concerned about teen experimentation than most parents. Parents often panic when they hear their child has smoked marijuana or taken alcohol from the cabinet. However, with education, guidance, and accountability, many teenagers drift away from early experimentation.

Substance use among adolescents and young adults has often been examined through a strict pathological lens. However, developmental research suggests that experimentation with substances can occur as part of broader identity exploration and social development during adolescence.

Developmental psychologist Jeffrey Arnett described this period as one characterized by identity exploration and experimentation, where young people assess boundaries and roles as they transition into adulthood (Arnett, 2005).

Within this context, limited experimentation with substances has been observed as relatively common behavior among adolescents navigating peer relationships, autonomy, and identity formation. Large national surveys consistently show that many adolescents report trying alcohol or other substances at least once before adulthood, reflecting the social and exploratory nature of this developmental stage (Johnston et al., 2023).

Researchers studying adolescent development note that risk-taking behaviors, including experimentation with substances, are partly influenced by neurological changes in the developing brain. During adolescence, reward-related brain systems develop more rapidly than the prefrontal cortex, which governs long-term decision-making and impulse control. This developmental imbalance increases sensitivity to novelty, reward, and peer influence (Steinberg, 2014; Casey, Jones, & Hare, 2008).

Importantly, most adolescents who experiment with substances do not develop long-term substance use disorders. Longitudinal studies indicate that many individuals "mature out" of risky substance use patterns as responsibilities, social roles, and cognitive control increase in adulthood (Winick, 1962; Schulenberg & Maggs, 2002).

These findings suggest that while substance use carries real health risks and should not be dismissed as harmless behavior, experimentation itself often occurs within broader developmental processes involving autonomy, peer belonging, and identity formation.

Substance Use

This is a hard area for me. I grew up many years without being around any substance abuse. Then, when I was in the ninth grade and moved to Kenmore schools, there was a lot of experimentation.

I know many kids who died from an overdose and were raised by parents who continued the legacy of addiction.

The problem is that people must want to quit, and many do not want to quit drinking or doing drugs. They consider it part of enjoying life.

This is a difficult reality. I have seen people addicted to pills—from Ambien to anxiety medications distributed throughout families. Many of these individuals were raised in environments where depression pills, anxiety pills, and sleeping pills were normalized.

They develop the mindset that if it is prescribed, it must be safe, not realizing that many of these medications are controlled substances.

Some individuals later develop dementia and long-term neurological side effects from prolonged use of certain sleeping pills, depression medications, and pain medications.

Research on Long-Term Medication Effects

I wrote this because I want others to be aware that Long-term use of certain medications commonly prescribed for sleep, anxiety, and chronic pain has been associated with increased risk of cognitive impairment and dementia, particularly among older adults.

Benzodiazepines, which are frequently prescribed for anxiety and insomnia, have been studied extensively in this context. Several large observational studies have found that prolonged benzodiazepine use is linked with higher rates of dementia and cognitive decline (Billioti de Gage et al., 2014; Islam et al., 2016). These medications can affect memory, attention, and neurological functioning, especially when used over extended periods.

Sedative-hypnotic medications commonly prescribed for sleep, such as zolpidem (Ambien), have also been associated with increased risk of cognitive impairment and neurological side effects when used chronically (Shih et al., 2015). Because these medications act on brain pathways that regulate sleep and sedation, long-term use can alter normal sleep architecture and the regulation of the nervous system.

Certain prescription pain medications, particularly opioids, have likewise been linked to cognitive decline when used over extended periods, as they affect central nervous system functioning and can impair attention, memory, and executive functioning (Schiltenwolf et al., 2014).

For this reason, many clinical guidelines recommend that medications for anxiety, sleep, and pain, especially benzodiazepines and sedative hypnotics, be used for short-term treatment, when possible, while emphasizing behavioral strategies, lifestyle changes, and psychosocial support for long-term management (American Geriatrics Society, 2019).

These findings do not mean that medication is inherently harmful. Many medications are helpful and appropriate when carefully monitored.

However, the research highlights the importance of cautious prescribing, patient education, and exploring long-term solutions that build resilience rather than dependence on sedative medications.

The Human Cost of Addiction

We do not understand how long-term substance use affects intimacy and relationships. It can leave individuals emotionally numb and disconnected from those around them.

Often, the root issue is never addressed.

Families suffer because the substance becomes more present than the relationships. Children, spouses, employers, parents, and friendships suffer the absence of the person who is physically there but emotionally unavailable.

Those outside the addiction often begin to question themselves, wondering if they are the problem.

If barriers and walls could be broken down, individuals might live in their fullness, thrive at work, build deep intimacy in relationships, and manifest families with healthy conversations.

The challenge is how to help individuals become free without attacking them.

Encouragement, accountability, and truth are often more effective than condemnation.

Sometimes people do not awaken until a crisis occurs, an accident, a loss, or a consequence that forces them to confront the reality of the addiction.

Treatment and Community

Substance use is one area where both systems are essential.

The treatment model is critical for withdrawal stabilization, relapse prevention, and safety. Clinical structure saves lives.

However, recovery rarely sustains without community.

Programs such as peer recovery groups demonstrate the power of shared testimony and accountability.

Many people drink or use substances to numb unresolved pain, shame, or early trauma.

Treatment interrupts the behavior.

Community rebuilds the person.

Treatment Model

- Diagnosing Substance Use Disorder

- Stabilize withdrawal

- Monitor relapse risk

Goal: Prevent harm.

Resilience Model

- Address shame

- Develop purpose

- Build an accountability community

- Rebuild relationships

Goal: Replace coping behavior with identity strength.

Treatment interrupts behavior.

Resilience rebuilds life.

Institutional Medication Culture and Intergenerational Dependence

We are on the verge of seeing a medication culture that is suffering through family systems.

I have seen relationships where grown men struggle to maintain healthy relationships because the atmosphere of the home was controlled by prescription medication. Medication became normalized as a daily routine. If someone felt sad or anxious, the response was simple: *take a pill.*

Substance patterns begin to shape the household's culture. Once individuals reach adulthood, this often becomes the default coping strategy. I have personally been in relationships like this that failed because the environment was so deeply embedded in these coping mechanisms that it seemed impossible to reverse.

After observing individuals who have suffered long-term effects from benzodiazepines and sedative medications, I have seen how these patterns can affect emotional development. Some individuals struggle to tolerate stress, engage in healthy conflict resolution, or regulate emotions without medication. In many cases, relationship skills and long-term resilience were never fully developed.

It is heartbreaking to watch people remain in cycles of survival mode, continually returning to the same coping strategies that shaped their early environments. These patterns can create intergenerational dependence, where the coping mechanisms of one generation become the behavioral template for the next.

I believe doctors, pharmaceutical systems, and communities should be better educated about the broader social effects of long-term prescription medication use. When certain medications are prescribed, especially benzodiazepines and sedative medications, patients and families should receive education about the potential long-term impacts not only on the individual but on the family environment and children growing up within that environment.

Open discussions within communities could raise awareness of these patterns. Educational systems, healthcare providers, and community programs could help families understand healthier coping strategies, breaking cycles that affect future generations and developing stronger emotional regulation and resilience.

Research on Medicalized Coping Culture

In many families, medication becomes normalized as the primary response to emotional distress, anxiety, insomnia, or trauma. Over time, this can create what some researchers describe as a medicalized coping culture, where prescription drugs become the default tool for managing psychological pain.

Studies show that parental use of prescription medications is associated with a higher likelihood of use among their children, pointing towards the fact that substance-use patterns can be transmitted through family environments and learned behavior. Children often observe medication use as a normal coping strategy and internalize the belief that distress should be managed through pharmaceuticals rather than relational or behavioral change.

This pattern is particularly significant with benzodiazepines and sedative medications commonly prescribed for anxiety, sleep, and stress, which have well-documented risks of tolerance, dependence, and misuse when used long-term. Research shows that medications such as benzodiazepines can lead to persistent use over time, with a massive portion of patients continuing to use long after the initial prescription period.

When these medications become embedded in family environments, they can shape attitudes about coping and emotional regulation. Individuals may begin to view prescription drugs as inherently safe simply because they are medically authorized.

However, many medications used for anxiety, sleep, and mood regulation are classified as controlled substances precisely because they carry dependence and addiction risks when misused or used long-term.

Research on the social ecology of substance use further shows that addiction and misuse rarely occur in isolation. Family systems, community norms, and access to substances all influence how individuals learn to cope with distress. When substance use—whether alcohol, illicit drugs, or prescription medication- becomes normalized within a household, it can create environments where reliance on substances persists across generations.

This does not mean medication itself is inherently harmful. Many medications are life-saving and appropriate when used carefully under medical supervision.

However, when pharmaceutical solutions replace relational support, mentorship, and community accountability, individuals may never develop the internal coping skills and relational structures necessary for long-term resilience.

In this sense, treatment can stabilize symptoms, but recovery and long-term health often depend on rebuilding the social and relational foundations that help people live without dependence.

Institutional Prevention Model

Because of these patterns, long-term prevention requires education across multiple systems.

Medical Education

- Increased education for physicians regarding long-term dependence risks

- Patient education when prescribing controlled medications

- Clear discussions about duration of use and alternatives

- Encouraging communication and healthy conflict resolution

- Building environments where distress is addressed relationally rather than chemically. Family education programs could require families to attend informational groups for continued medication use, in addition to returning unused medication. • Teaching emotional regulation and coping skills within families.

Community and Pharmaceutical Awareness

- Community discussions about medication culture and resilience

- Collaboration between healthcare providers and community support systems

- Increased emphasis on behavioral, relational, and community-based support

Goal: Reduce intergenerational dependence on medication-based coping and strengthen long-term resilience within families and communities.

The Core Distinction

Treatment asks:

How do we reduce symptoms and prevent harm?

Resilience asks:

How do we grow stronger through this struggle?

Treatment is short-term stabilization.

Resilience is a long-term formation.

Treatment is clinical.

Resilience is relational.

Treatment manages risk.

Resilience builds identity.

Clinical treatment is essential when there is severe impairment, danger, or a psychiatric disorder.

Resilience work is essential when growth, development, and relational distress coexist.

They are not enemies.

However, they serve distinct roles.

When we confuse those roles, we overload the clinical system and underfund the very community structures that build long-term strength.

That distinction is where reform begins.

BRIDGE TO CHAPTER 8
DRAWING THE BOUNDARY

Who Needs Clinical Care?

If every human struggle is treated as a disorder, the system eventually loses the ability to distinguish between crisis and development.

Clinical care is essential for severe mental illness, dangerous impairment, and conditions that require medical stabilization. However, when diagnosis becomes the default response to grief, conflict, identity development, or relational pain, the clinical system begins carrying responsibilities it was never designed to hold.

The result is not only an overwhelmed system, but communities that slowly lose their role in forming resilient individuals.

To restore balance, we must ask a difficult but necessary question:

Who needs clinical care?

CHAPTER 8

DRAWING THE BOUNDARY

WHERE DO WE DRAW THE LINE?

One of the hardest questions in understanding human struggle is this: Where do we draw the line between someone who needs mentorship and someone who needs clinical mental health care?

Real life does not present itself in neat categories.

Sometimes the signs are obvious.

Sometimes they are not.

Consider the family where parents are exhausted from dealing with a teenager who steals money, takes the car without permission, sneaks out at night, refuses to do homework, and shows no respect for boundaries.

The parents eventually reach a breaking point.

Arguments escalate.

Voices get louder.

Anger grows.

Soon, the household is filled with yelling, accusations, and verbal attacks. The family system becomes chaotic. Everyone is reacting instead of leading. Drama surrounds the home and begins to define the relationships within it.

In another home, the problem looks different.

The husband and father drink excessively. When he begins drinking, he cannot stop. Alcohol controls the evening. Family members hold their breath while he drives home, silently thanking God that he made it home without hurting himself or someone else.

The family lives around his addiction.

Another family struggles differently.

Prescription medications circulate through the household. Pills are shared, borrowed, and redistributed among family members as if nothing is wrong. What began as medical treatment slowly becomes chemical dependence that affects the entire family system.

In some relationships, the struggle becomes explosive.

Couples scream at each other in anger.

Arguments escalate into verbal abuse.

Sometimes they become physical.

These are not isolated problems affecting one individual.

They are systems of dysfunction.

Over time, families living in these environments adapt to the chaos.

What once seemed alarming begins to feel normal.

Roles become distorted.

Boundaries collapse.

Responsibility becomes unclear.

So, the question remains:

Where do we draw the line?

When does someone need mentorship, accountability, and community guidance?

When does someone need clinical mental health intervention?

Another difficult question follows close behind.

What happens when someone is willing to get help, open to growth, ready to change, and capable of reflection?

What happens when someone has no self-awareness at all?

Some individuals can look honestly at their lives and say:

"I need help."

"I need to change."

"I need guidance."

These individuals may benefit from mentorship, community support, accountability, and relational guidance.

However, others are unable to see the problem.

They deny it.

They deflect it.

They blame others.

Without self-awareness, meaningful change becomes extremely difficult.

This is where the distinction begins to emerge.

Mentorship works best when a person has some level of awareness and willingness to grow.

Clinical care becomes essential when a person's behaviors, thinking patterns, addictions, emotional regulation, or psychological stability prevent them from functioning safely or responsibly.

Understanding this difference is not about labelling people as good or bad.

It is about recognizing the type of help that will need to change.

Not every struggle requires clinical intervention.

Some situations clearly do.

The challenge for families, communities, churches, and professionals is learning how to recognize the difference.

That question sits at the center of this chapter.

Another difficult reality must also be acknowledged.

What about the people who never seem to change?

The ones who have been using the same drugs since high school and are still living the exact same life decades later.

The individuals who talk about the same problems ten years later as if nothing has ever shifted.

The same complaints.

The same conflicts.

The same stories.

The same wounds replayed repeatedly.

What about the individuals who seem trapped in the same poverty cycle year after year?

No matter how many opportunities appear, they seem unable to move forward.

Life becomes a constant struggle just to stay afloat.

Then there are those whose lives seem surrounded by continual sickness and loss.

One crisis after another.

One tragedy after another.

Their lives appear to move from hardship to hardship without recovery in between.

And then there are the relational patterns that drain everyone around them.

The individuals who are constantly taking but never giving.

The people who absorb the energy of every room they enter.

Conversations revolve around them.

Problems revolve around them.

The needs of others rarely appear in the picture.

Sometimes these patterns go even further.

There are individuals who manipulate others financially, emotionally, or relationally.

Some embezzle.

Some deceive.

Some exploit the trust of the people around them.

These are not simply difficult seasons of life.

These are patterns.

Patterns that repeat for years.

Sometimes for decades.

So, the question becomes even more complex.

When does someone need community mentorship, accountability, and relational support?

When does someone need clinical mental health care?

Community can guide people who are willing to grow.

Mentorship can help people who are open to correction.

Relationships can help individuals who are capable of reflection and change.

However, when patterns become deeply entrenched—when addictions persist, when destructive behaviors repeat, when self-awareness is absent, and when accountability is consistently rejected, the situation may move beyond what the community alone can address.

Clinical mental health systems exist for a reason.

They provide structure, stabilization, and treatment for individuals whose behaviors, emotional regulation, addictions, or psychological conditions involve professional intervention.

The community cannot force transformation on someone who refuses to change.

Mentorship cannot help someone who rejects accountability.

Relationships cannot repair patterns that someone refuses to examine.

Drawing the boundary requires discernment.

Some people need guidance.

Some people need treatment.

Some people need both.

Understanding that difference is not about judgment.

It is about recognizing what kind of help a person truly needs.

Without that clarity, we risk sending people to systems that cannot solve the problem.

Community cannot replace clinical care for severe impairment.

Clinical care cannot replace the community's role in shaping identity, purpose, and belonging.

Both have their place.

However, knowing when one is needed more than the other is one of the most important boundaries we must learn to recognize.

One of the most important questions facing modern communities is this:

Who needs clinical mental health care?

Not every human struggle is a mental illness.

Some individuals require professional clinical treatment because their psychological condition severely impairs their ability to function safely and independently.

However, many people seeking guidance are not suffering from psychiatric illness.

They are navigating the normal challenges of human growth—developing identity, learning accountability, building relationships, and discovering purpose.

When we fail to distinguish between these two realities, we risk medicalizing normal human development while leaving communities without the structures necessary to support growth, belonging, and resilience.

Understanding this boundary is essential.

Without clarity, normal human development can be labeled as illness, while individuals experiencing severe psychological impairment may not receive the focused care they truly need.

People Who Do Not Need Clinical Care

The ones who do not need clinical care are those who want to build normal, healthy growth, purpose, establish identity, and build deeper relationships with accountability. I am a person who loves to grow from my mistakes and loves a relationship that is a challenge. I always outgrow people, because I am always chasing after God and seeking more wisdom and knowledge. There is a price to pay for growth, and often you outgrow people. A lot of people want to stay comfortable and not change.

Many individuals seeking guidance are not suffering from mental illness; however, they are experiencing normal stages of human growth and development. Psychological research shows that healthy people often pursue personal responsibility, purpose, and self-improvement as part of internal and psychological well-being. Theories of self-actualization, resilience, and human development suggest that struggles related to identity, relationships, and life transitions are often part of normal development rather than psychiatric disorders (Maslow, 1968; Ryff, 1989; Deci & Ryan, 2000; Erikson, 1968).

These individuals are more likely to thrive through mentorship, community support, and personal growth opportunities than through clinical treatment.

I have also witnessed young individuals in their twenties. They have no kids, they do not want to get in trouble, and they are going to college or just starting their own businesses. However, there is nothing in the community for these young individuals to do besides going to bars and dating sites, and they end up feeling lonely. I know this because I have had these individuals who want someone to spend time with, whether that is sitting and talking or going out to eat.

I am at a different stage in my life with kids, so many of these girls want to spend time with me while I am raising children. The sad part is that they are so desperate to get out and do something that they get coerced into going to bars, end up going out with a guy they should not, or find themselves pulled into chaotic relationships because there are no healthy community options available to them.

Then they find themselves getting an OUI, and it is heartbreaking to watch.

These are not individuals suffering from mental illness.

These are individuals seeking a sense of belonging, direction, and purpose.

What they need is community.

We need to reinvent the community for this age group.

- Spaces for belonging.

- Identity-building

- Empowerment

- Mentorship

- Purpose

When healthy individuals have no place to grow, no mentors to guide them, and no community that cultivates identity and responsibility, they often end up searching for belonging in places that harm them.

Growth Through Conflict and Communication

I know I grow through resilience and hardships. I always say to God, I know when I come out of this hurt, I will see things differently. Many people who learn resilience through hardships show grace to others and can see the blessing that comes from something that appears extremely bad after they come through it. Conflict resolution can foster deeper inner growth in a relationship, and communication can help build greater intimacy.

Healthy communication and constructive conflict resolution can strengthen intimacy in relationships. When partners discuss disagreements openly, listen respectfully, and work together to find solutions, they build trust, understanding, and emotional closeness (Gottman & Levenson, 1999; Canary & Dindia, 2013).

Many individuals and couples want to accomplish this at the highest level so they can continue to grow. Individuals need to know where they are in terms of self-awareness and take a self-assessment.

Who Needs Clinical Care?

Clinical mental health treatment is critical for individuals experiencing severe psychological impairment that significantly affects their ability to function safely or independently.

Conditions such as major depressive disorder with suicidal thoughts, psychotic disorders, severe bipolar disorder, debilitating trauma, and serious anxiety disorders often require professional assessment, diagnosis, and clinical intervention. Mental health professionals are trained to stabilize symptoms, manage risk, and provide evidence-based treatment for these conditions.

Research in psychiatry and clinical psychology emphasizes that untreated severe mental illness can lead to serious impairment in relationships, work, and daily functioning, making professional care essential for safety and recovery (American Psychiatric Association, 2022; Insel, 2010; National Institute of Mental Health, 2023).

When Lack of Growth Becomes a Pattern

When a lack of growth becomes a pattern, individuals become less open to self-awareness, growth, and accountability. They may refuse clinical mental health counseling, or the community might help them open up. Research in psychology and relationship studies shows that when individuals are not open to self-awareness, growth, or accountability, relationships often experience ongoing conflict, emotional distance, and instability. A closed mindset can make it difficult for partners to accept feedback, recognize their role in problems, or adapt their behavior.

Over time, this can lead to repeated arguments, unresolved resentment, and reduced trust between partners.

Studies on relationship dynamics show that couples who avoid accountability and responsibility, or who refuse to reflect on their own behavior, often become trapped in negative communication patterns such as blame, defensiveness, and criticism. These patterns are strongly associated with lower relationship satisfaction and higher rates of separation or divorce (Gottman & Levenson, 1999).

Psychologist Carol Dweck also found that individuals with a fixed mindset, believing that people cannot change or grow, are more likely to avoid personal responsibility and struggle with conflict resolution, which can weaken relationships over time (Dweck, 2006).

At the same time, individuals who practice self-awareness and personal accountability are more likely to repair conflict, build trust, and develop a deeper emotional connection.

A lack of self-awareness, accountability, and openness to growth can damage relationships by increasing conflict, defensiveness, and emotional distance. Research shows that closed-mindedness and avoidance of responsibility are associated with lower relationship satisfaction and greater difficulty resolving conflict (Gottman & Levenson, 1999; Dweck, 2006).

I have seen moments where self-awareness begins to break through, even in exceedingly difficult situations. When pride softens, and people are willing to admit they are broken, something powerful can begin.

I once spoke with a woman who was in a relationship with the father of her three children. Both were seeking God and had chosen to live celibately because they believed it was an act of faith, and they were not married. Yet their relationship was full of confusion and pain.

She longed for emotional connection, affection, and friendship from him. Coming from a broken family history in which she had often been the caretaker, she brought her emotions heavily into the relationship. She wanted reassurance and closeness every day.

The man she loved had grown up surrounded by addiction. Drinking had become the only way he knew how to cope with stress and conflict. He also carried a long struggle with pornography that began in childhood, something he deeply hated about himself but felt powerless to stop.

She believed his lack of affection meant he did not love her.

He believed he was constantly falling short of her expectations.

Both were wounded in separate ways.

He did not yet have the emotional health to offer the affection she needed.

She had never been taught how to communicate her emotions healthily.

Neither of them was a villain.

Both were carrying patterns shaped by their families and past experiences.

What stood out to me was how quickly they grasped the importance of self-awareness. Instead of endlessly blaming each other, they began asking each other questions and learning about each other.

She started writing daily reflections and exercises, asking herself how she could change her mindset instead of trying to control the relationship. She began learning how to release the constant monitoring of his behavior and focus on her own growth.

He openly admitted something important: "I know it is wrong, but I do not know how to stop."

That statement revealed an essential conviction.

Conviction and self-awareness are often the first signs that growth is possible. Without them, people remain trapped in defensiveness, blame, and denial.

When someone becomes willing to look honestly at themselves, the possibility of change begins.

Psychological research describes this moment as the beginning of self-awareness when individuals recognize the gap between their behavior and their values. In Christian theology, this same moment is often described as conviction—the work of the Holy Spirit awakening the conscience and leading a person toward repentance and transformation.

Hopeless Depression and A Need for Community

People who have no hope need community, and sometimes they also need clinical mental health services that encourage them back toward community.

I have sat with individuals who are older and struggling with depression. Many of them have had depression their entire lives. When looking back over their lives, many say they were satisfied with their jobs, they felt purpose, they had husbands or wives, and they built families. However, now those things are gone.

When I ask what they want right now, I often hear the same answers:

"I want a companion."

"I want a husband."

"I want a wife."

"I want someone to do something with."

They want purpose again, but many of them cannot reflect on the past and see a continued meaningful life purpose as they get older.

Instead, they are slowly fading away through depression medication that is not working, while continuing to see counselors who say they are trying different approaches with them. These individuals are tired. Instead of reflecting on their accomplishments, they still feel unsatisfied.

One day, I asked a woman a simple question:

"What if there were a community meeting space where elders could meet and communicate?"

She responded immediately.

"Well, I would not go."

I asked her why.

"Well, I would not go by myself."

Then I asked another question.

"Are you okay with meeting people on Facebook by yourself?"

That made her stop and think.

Then I said something else to her.

"I wonder if you could mentor younger women."

She responded,

"Well, my niece… it is nice to meet up with her sometimes, but she does not need me."

In that moment, it hit me deeply.

I felt bad for this woman because she was precious and needed more than she could ever know from the community. Her wisdom, her knowledge, and the way she had managed two long marriages and the loss of both husbands was a powerful testimony that could help so many other people.

Depression often makes people feel hopeless and pessimistic.

However, in my mind, as a younger woman sitting there, I was thinking something completely different.

I need you.

I need your wisdom.

I need your knowledge.

I need your life experience.

I said something very direct to her that day.

"You are comfortable. You say you want change, but you do not want to step outside of your comfort zone."

"You want your health issues taken care of, but you will not try something in the community. Because those options are not available, you continue going to doctors and hoping someone there will fix what you are feeling.

She paused and then said something surprising.

She agreed with me.

That moment raised a question that has stayed with me ever since.

When will a clinical mental health counselor say to someone:

"You need a mentor. You need purpose. You need relationships. Here are the programs and people in the community who can help you find that."

A clinical mental health counselor could refer individuals to community resources, mentorship opportunities, or even elders' groups within churches where wisdom and relationships are valued.

For someone like this woman, that kind of connection might replace the hopelessness of depression with something entirely different.

Hope.

Hope that she still has purpose.

Hope that her life experience still matters.

I hope that her story helps others.

Scripture speaks directly about this kind of hope.

1 Thessalonians 5:8 say:

"But since we belong to the day, let us be sober, putting on faith and love as a breastplate, and the hope of salvation as a helmet."

Hope protects the mind.

Sometimes the path back to hope begins not with another diagnosis, but with community, purpose, and relationships that remind a person that their life still matters.

Hopelessness and Psychological Research

Research shows that persistent pessimism and hopelessness are strongly associated with depression. Psychological theories such as hopelessness theory and learned helplessness suggest that when individuals believe their future cannot improve and their actions have an insignificant impact, they are more likely to develop depressive symptoms (Beck, 1967; Seligman, 1975).

With the help of clinical mental health systems, pointing individuals toward community involvement can help them toward restoration.

These individuals are often in a state of slumber.

Long-Term Treatment Without Growth

Some individuals remain in long-term treatment routines without moving toward broader life change because of factors such as treatment dependency, learned helplessness, or avoidance coping.

Research shows that when individuals believe change is difficult or risky, they may remain within familiar therapeutic structures rather than engage the challenges of personal growth and community participation (Seligman, 1975; Herman, 1992).

Treatment Dependency

Some researchers describe this as treatment dependency, where a person becomes reliant on therapy or clinical systems for ongoing support without developing independence or broader life change.

Learned Helplessness

Psychologist Martin Seligman studied learned helplessness, where individuals believe they have little control over improving their situation (Seligman, 1975).

Comfort Zone/Avoid Coping

Individuals stay within routines that reduce anxiety but prevent growth.

Institutionalization

Long-term reliance on structured systems can lead to institutionalization, in which individuals struggle to function outside the system.

When Clinical Treatment Is Necessary

Research in psychology suggests that individuals who repeatedly remain stuck in destructive routines and struggle to change their behavior may require clinical mental health support.

Psychologists describe these patterns through concepts such as learned helplessness, fixed mindset, and behavioral rigidity.

Psychologist Martin Seligman developed the theory of learned helplessness, explaining how individuals can stop attempting change altogether (Seligman, 1975).

Similarly, Carol Dweck's research on mindset shows that individuals who believe that change is impossible often repeat destructive patterns rather than develop healthier perspectives (Dweck, 2006).

Psychologists also describe behavioral rigidity, where individuals struggle to adapt their thinking or behavior when circumstances change.

When these patterns become severe, they may reflect deeper emotional or psychological distress such as depression, trauma, or personality disorders.

Clinical mental health treatment can help individuals recognize destructive patterns, develop self-awareness, learn healthier coping skills, and build the capacity for change.

Personal Observation

I have collaborated with individuals who exhibit these patterns. They return to counseling repeatedly, repeating the same conversations about the same problems.

At times, I could not believe it.

We would talk about the same issue for months, sometimes for an entire year, without making any progress.

There were moments when I would say,

"Can't we move past this?

Can't you forgive her?

Can't we start focusing on something new?"

However, the conversation kept returning to the same subject.

It was like being stuck in a loop.

I noticed that for some people, their thinking becomes so rigid that growth almost feels impossible.

The same wounds, the same arguments, and the same interpretations repeat themselves over and over.

I do not fully know how these rigid mindsets form.

I often realize they began much earlier in life, through childhood neglect, unresolved pain, or environments where emotional development never fully matured.

I began noticing the same patterns outside of counseling as well.

People I knew from high school were still the same years later.

Relationships where progress was made one day, but the very next day, the person reverted to the same behavior.

Friendships where you tried to hold someone accountable, but instead of reflecting, they twisted the truth or refused to take responsibility.

Accountability felt almost impossible.

Then I met someone else who seemed different. At first, I believed this individual was finally emerging from the institutional mindset and beginning to grow.

There were moments where I thought real change was happening.

Then weeks would pass without speaking, and when we talked again, it was as if all progress had disappeared. The same behavioral patterns returned.

In fact, sometimes it felt as if the person had taken ten steps backward instead of forward.

That was when something became clear to me.

For some individuals, the structure and routine of clinical mental health services may be necessary for their stability. Removing that structure too quickly or expecting them to function within community mentorship alone immediately could be more disturbing than helpful.

Not everyone is ready for the same kind of support.

Some people truly need the consistency and structure of clinical care because their thinking patterns, emotional regulation, or behavioral cycles are deeply ingrained.

Understanding that distinction is important.

Community mentorship can help many people grow.

For others, clinical mental health services remain an essential support system that provides the stability they need. For some individuals, the structure and routine of clinical mental health services may be necessary for their stability. Removing that structure too quickly or expecting them to function within community mentorship alone immediately could be more disturbing than helpful.

Not everyone is ready for the same kind of support.

Some people truly need the consistency and structure of clinical care because their thinking patterns, emotional regulation, or behavioral cycles are deeply ingrained.

Understanding that distinction is important.

It is also important to acknowledge a painful reality. When growth begins in one person but not the other, relationships can begin to shift. Sometimes couples outgrow one another. Friendships may slowly fade when one person develops self-awareness while the other remains unable or unwilling to reflect on their behavior.

Growth changes people. Without mutual reflection and accountability, relationships can become strained or even dissolve.

This is often why counselors find themselves repeating the same conversations with clients who are not yet ready to accept responsibility for their role in the problem. Until accountability appears, progress can remain limited.

Community mentorship can help many people grow.

However, for others, clinical mental health services remain an essential support system that provides the stability they need.

Drawing The Boundary

These experiences helped me understand something important: not every human struggle belongs in the same category.

Some individuals need mentorship, accountability, and community to grow. Others need the stabilization and structure that clinical mental health systems provide.

When these boundaries are not clearly understood, confusion begins.

Healthy people who are simply searching for identity, relationships, and purpose can become trapped in systems designed for illness.

At the same time, individuals who truly need clinical care may be pushed too quickly into environments that do not provide the structure they require.

This is why discernment matters.

Clinical mental health has a key role when people are experiencing severe emotional impairment, long-standing psychological patterns, or conditions that require structured treatment and stabilization.

Nevertheless, the community also has an essential role. Community provides belonging, accountability, mentorship, and purpose, things that institutions alone cannot create.

When both systems remain in their proper place, people receive the support they need.

Clinical care stabilizes the mind when illness is present.

Community builds identity, relationships, and purpose.

Understanding where one ends and the other begins is one of the most important boundaries our society must learn to recognize.

Research therefore suggests that while many people experience normal struggles that can be addressed through community support, mentorship, or personal growth, individuals who remain trapped in rigid behavioral cycles and cannot move toward accountability or change may benefit from structured clinical mental health care.

Professional therapy provides tools for breaking entrenched patterns, addressing underlying psychological conditions, and helping individuals regain the ability to function and grow (Seligman, 1975; Dweck, 2006).

The Boundary Between Clinical Care and Community

Drawing this boundary clearly is essential for both individuals and communities.

Many people seeking guidance are not suffering from mental illness. They are navigating the normal challenges of human development, learning accountability, building identity, developing relationships, and pursuing purpose. These individuals often benefit most from mentorship, community relationships, spiritual growth, and environments that encourage responsibility and personal development.

At the same time, there are individuals whose psychological patterns prevent them from moving forward on their own. When a person becomes trapped in rigid behavioral cycles, persistent hopelessness, or severe emotional impairment that disrupts daily functioning, clinical mental health care becomes necessary. In these situations, professional treatment can help stabilize symptoms, develop self-awareness, and provide structured tools for breaking destructive patterns.

The danger arises when these two realities become confused.

When normal human struggles are treated primarily as medical conditions, individuals who need guidance, mentorship, and community may begin to see themselves as patients rather than as developing human beings.

At the same time, when severe psychological impairment is not recognized, individuals who truly require clinical intervention may remain trapped in patterns that continue to harm their lives and relationships.

Understanding the difference protects both systems.

Clinical mental health care exists to stabilize severe psychological conditions and help individuals regain functioning.

Community exists to cultivate identity, purpose, accountability, and belonging.

When these roles work together rather than replacing one another, individuals are far more likely to experience both healing and growth.

Drawing this boundary allows clinical care to focus on those who truly need it while restoring the community's role in helping people develop resilience, relationships, and purpose.

The Third Dimension: Spiritual Transformation

When we talk about drawing the boundary between clinical care and community mentorship, another dimension must also be recognized.

Human beings are not only psychological and social beings.

They are also spiritual beings.

For some people, the deepest transformation in their lives does not come from therapy or from community programs. It comes from a spiritual encounter that reshapes their identity, their purpose, and the condition of their heart.

Clinical care can stabilize mental illness.

Community can provide a sense of belonging, mentorship, accountability, and relationships.

Spiritual transformation addresses something deeper.

It addresses the soul.

Throughout history, many people have experienced profound change through faith, repentance, forgiveness, and a renewed sense of identity through God. These experiences cannot always be explained through clinical frameworks or social environments alone.

That does not mean every struggle is spiritual.

Some situations require professional medical care.

Some require mentorship and relational support.

Ignoring the spiritual dimension of human life leaves a significant part of the human experience unexplained.

For some people, transformation begins when they encounter God and begin a personal relationship with Him.

That is where my story begins.

Personal Testimony

For me personally, it was not community programs or clinical mental health services that transformed my life.

It was my surrender to God.

It was when I began a personal relationship with Him and received the Holy Spirit that the real transformation began.

The change was real.

At times, it looked strange to others. I went through a deep transformation that people around me did not always understand.

I went from vanity and ego to learning self-love through God.

I went from seeking attention to learning vulnerability, loving others, and serving others.

My heart softened.

Instead of defending myself or blaming others, I began holding myself accountable for my actions.

The hardened heart I once had begun to change.

I went from being a woman in the world ruled by performance to becoming a woman humbled by the love of God and called to help lead others to Christ.

However, the process was not easy.

Transformation rarely is.

Many people did not understand my dreams, my visions, or my deep love for God. At times, I wished churches understood this process better or that I had a strong mentor guiding me through it.

Instead, many of the mentors I found were elders in homes. Some were former pastors' wives who spoke wisdom into my life.

My mother was one of my greatest mentors.

My father never left my side.

He often showed up with me when I visited new churches, supporting me as I searched for where I belonged.

The transformation of my mindset took years.

For a long time, it was just me, God, and the Word of God working through that process.

I did attend a Saturday church service for many years, but eventually that church became very institutionalized.

Faith also requires discernment.

Not every spiritual environment is healthy. Some religious environments can become controlling or cult-like, and it is important to recognize when people are being spiritually harmed or misled.

I once encountered a woman who believed she was Jesus Christ and had been sent here to die on the cross. Situations like that remind us that not every spiritual experience reflects truth or health.

Discernment matters.

My larger point is this:

Some people are going through deep transformation because God is working in their lives.

When someone begins that journey, they often need guidance from someone who understands faith and spiritual growth.

Without a Christian mentor or pastoral guidance, people going through spiritual transformation can feel isolated or misunderstood, especially when they are surrounded by people who do not share their beliefs.

This is where pastoral counseling can play a vital role.

Pastoral counseling can guide people through the difficult but powerful process of spiritual transformation.

The process can be challenging.

The power of God is real.

During my years working as a counselor, and even today, I visit many churches to help guide people toward communities where they may feel spiritually connected.

Through all my years of counseling, I have met many individuals and couples who deeply desired their relationship with God to grow.

This is especially important for couples seeking Christian counseling.

When couples want their relationship centered on faith, counseling must be grounded in God, with the understanding that God comes first in the relationship.

Faith cannot simply be added as an afterthought.

It must be the foundation. Because of that, discernment becomes essential.

The Boundary That Must Be Recognized

As we begin to understand human struggle more clearly, three distinct areas emerge.

Clinical mental health care exists to stabilize psychological illness, addiction, and severe impairment. It provides structure, treatment, and professional intervention when someone's thinking, emotions, or behaviors prevent them from functioning safely or responsibly.

Community provides something different. Community builds belonging, mentorship, accountability, identity, and relational support. It helps people grow through connection, responsibility, and shared life.

Nevertheless, there is also a third dimension that cannot be ignored.

Spiritual transformation.

For some people, the deepest changes in their lives occur when their identity is restored through faith and their hearts are transformed by their relationship with God.

These three systems serve separate roles.

Clinical care stabilizes illness.

Community builds belonging and purpose.

Faith transforms identity and the human heart.

When these roles become confused, systems begin carrying responsibilities they were never designed to hold.

Clinical care cannot replace community.

Community cannot replace spiritual transformation.

Faith cannot replace medical care when illness is present.

When each one functions in its proper place, people receive the kind of help that truly leads to healing, growth, and transformation.

Recognizing these boundaries is not about dividing people.

It is about understanding the diverse ways human beings heal, grow, and change.

Learning to recognize those differences may be one of the most important responsibilities our society faces today.

Clinical care stabilizes the mind.

Community builds identity and belonging.

Faith transforms the heart.

When we understand the difference, we begin to restore what has been lost.

PART IV

UNDERSTANDING THE CONFUSION

CHAPTER 9

THE EXPOSURE PROBLEM

Because they are overloaded and influenced by things that distort reality. Because they are overloaded and influenced by things that distort reality.

Today, we are exposed to more information than any generation before us, and our minds were never designed for it. Research shows that constant exposure to enormous amounts of information, especially through social media and news, can overwhelm our cognitive system and increase anxiety.

In earlier times, people dealt with immediate, local concerns: food, shelter, safety, and survival. The threats they faced were real, present, and directly connected to their daily lives. Information was limited to their environment and community.

I did not learn this in a classroom; I learned it in living rooms.

The more time I spent in people's homes, the more I began to see patterns. What people allowed into their environments was shaping how they felt, thought, and functioned.

In some homes, the news played constantly in the background, filling the space with fear, crisis, and negativity. In others, phones and screens dominated attention, endless scrolling, social media, and content that created distractions and disconnection.

I witnessed how certain forms of entertainment, including unrealistic images and false representations of life, began to interfere with real relationships, marriages, and identity.

This included exposure to highly stimulating and unrealistic content, including pornography, which is increasingly influencing how individuals view relationships.

Research shows that repeated exposure to this type of content can affect the brain's reward system, increase dopamine-driven responses while reducing sensitivity to real-life connections and intimacy.

Over time, this can lead to emotional detachment, unrealistic expectations, and decreased satisfaction in real relationships.

Instead of emotionally working through conflict, communicating, and growing within relationships, some individuals begin to rely on artificial alternatives that feel easier and more immediately rewarding.

It becomes a replacement rather than a solution. This weakens emotional depth and creates relationships that lack connection, effort, and authenticity.

This is not limited to men or women; it affects both. People begin to compare their relationships, their bodies, and their lives to something that is not real. What they are consuming begins to redefine what they expect.

These were not isolated situations. They were consistent.

People were being influenced daily by what they consumed—often without realizing it.

Today, we are constantly taking in information from everywhere, wars, disasters, conflicts, and crises from across the world. Even when these events have no direct impact on our lives, our brains still process them as potential threats.

Psychologists have identified this as information overload, a condition where the brain becomes overwhelmed by the volume of input it is trying to process. This leads to mental fatigue, anxiety, and reduced clarity.

Research also shows that heavy social media use contributes to a phenomenon called social media fatigue, which drains cognitive energy and increases emotional instability. Constant exposure to news, especially through digital platforms, has been linked to higher levels of stress, anxiety, and emotional strain over time.

In other words, the brain becomes overwhelmed, not because of immediate danger, but because it is trying to process too much at once.

We are not just dealing with our own lives; we are carrying the emotional weight of the entire world.

The human brain struggles to distinguish between what is happening nearby and what is happening far away. As a result, we respond emotionally to events we cannot control, creating a constant internal state of stress.

At the same time, we are surrounded by the illusion of connection. Social media presents carefully constructed versions of people's lives, leading us to compare ourselves to unrealistic standards. Appearances, lifestyles, and identities are filtered and curated, yet we internalize them as reality.

This creates confusion.

People begin to believe they should look, live, or feel a certain way. They begin to measure their lives against something that is not fully real.

These are not true relationships. These are not the people who will show up in real life. Yet they influence identity, self-worth, and perception.

When the world becomes too loud, the individual begins to lose clarity.

This is not because people are weak. It is because they are overwhelmed.

We are also living in a culture where external messaging reinforces this overload, constant advertisements, including those related to health and medication, normalize the idea that distress is something to be immediately treated rather than understood.

Without awareness, people begin to believe the problem is entirely within them, rather than recognizing that the environment influences them.

There needs to be more education around this.

The human mind has limits. When those limits are exceeded, it leads to overload, fatigue, anxiety, and confusion.

We are not just facing new problems; we are facing a new level of exposure that our minds were never built to handle.

And without understanding this, we risk mislabeling overload as disorder and influence as identity.

- The brain was designed for limited, local input.

- Modern life = constant, global exposure

- Overexposure leads to:

Anxiety

Fatigue

Confusion

Pornography & hyper-stimulating content:

Alter reward.

Reduce real connection.

Social media:

Creates an illusion of connection.

Increase comparison.

News:

Creates fear of distant threats.

The environment shapes identity more than people realize.

Fake input = fake expectations

Too much input = overwhelmed brain

Overwhelmed brain = confused identity

What We Fail to Teach

If we are going to address the confusion, anxiety, and disconnection we are seeing today, then we must change what we are teaching. The problem is not just within individuals; it is within what they are exposed to and what they are never taught to understand.

We are not teaching individuals how their environment alters their mind, how constant exposure shape's identity, or how to recognize the distinction between reality and illusion.

If we do not teach this, we will continue to misinterpret overload as disorder and influence as identity.

How do media, social media, porn, and news impact the brain?

How it contributes to anxiety, confusion, and identity distortion

How to recognize unhealthy inputs and begin reducing them.

"People are not just struggling internally."

They are overloaded and influenced by what they consume."

What We Need to Teach

How exposure affects the brain and emotions

The difference between real connection and digital interaction

How social media creates comparison and distorted identity.

How explicit content influences expectations and relationships

Including pornography

How constant news exposure increases fear and anxiety.

How to recognize when the mind is overloaded

How to reduce unhealthy input and rebuild clarity.

This is not about removing everything.

 It is about being aware of what is influencing you.

CHAPTER 10

WHERE THE CONFUSION COMES IN

I remember standing in my client's kitchen when I asked her what she had been diagnosed with during her counseling.

She told me she had not been diagnosed with her marriage counseling.

I asked her if she used insurance.

She said yes.

I said, "Then both you and your husband were diagnosed."

She continued to argue with me for a while, but eventually I explained how the system works.

I have another friend who has been seeing a mental health counselor.

I asked her what she was diagnosed with.

She said, "Oh, I do not think she diagnosed me."

I said, "If you are using Medicaid, she most certainly did."

I often think to myself, how do people not know?

It is very confusing to me when a married couple does not realize they are being assessed or diagnosed, or when a young woman has no idea that a diagnosis has been placed in her file.

Not to mention when a teenager struggles with identity and is sent to counseling.

An adult uses insurance for therapy but cannot explain their diagnosis.

A community program meant to build mentorship is evaluated using clinical standards.

Somewhere along the way, the lines between treatment, development, and belonging began to blur.

Once those boundaries blur, confusion spreads through families, schools, funding systems, and culture itself.

What is even more confusing is seeing families continue using controlled substances intended for short-term use, yet remain unaware, shaped by the values and morals they were raised with, and see no right or wrong in it.

Teenagers who are suffering from isolation and elders who are mistreated or abused often have no real advocates for them, only nurses and mental health services.

Many of them do not need mental health treatment.

They need protectors.

They need advocates.

Another serious issue arises when clients mistake caseworkers for counselors, when mental health providers share personal phone numbers, or when providers cross clear ethical boundaries, even engaging in inappropriate relationships with clients.

I have also seen situations where supervisors have no one legally above them to hold them accountable for their decisions regarding interns or billing practices.

Even more troubling is the marketing of diagnoses in STEM schools, where innocent children are labeled too quickly.

Another confusing reality is that it often feels like clinical mental health services are the only option people have for counseling.

Because of legal restrictions, many people cannot even use the word "counselor" unless they hold a specific license.

You can become a pastoral counselor, but that often leaves individuals feeling like their only option outside of the clinical system is the church.

When we search online for help, why are most of the available services still categorized under mental health?

Why does funding seem to focus only on job development, education, and poverty-mindset programs?

Why can't funding support relationship building, communication skills, workplace empowerment, tools for stronger marriages, celebrations that bring people together, or creativity workshops that help people build identity?

Why can't there be the building blocks of a healthy community instead of constantly focusing on sickness?

It is deeply concerning when individuals claim they were never diagnosed, despite using insurance or Medicaid for counseling, yet cannot identify what their diagnosis was.

If a person has been labeled, billed, and medicated, yet cannot identify the condition they were treated for, what does that reveal about accountability in the system?

When categorization becomes procedural rather than relational, confusion spreads.

I see the same confusion in our schools.

Teenagers are sometimes threatened with being sent to a mental health counselor as if something must be wrong with them.

The message may not always be spoken directly, but it is clearly felt:

Struggle equals defect.

When can teenagers feel that what they are going through might be normal?

At what point do parents recognize that normal developmental struggles are not always disorders?

Adolescence becomes pathology.

Identity formation becomes disorder.

At the same time, many parents are overwhelmed and afraid.

Instead of slowing down to guide development, families often compensate by filling their lives with busyness, sports, band, and nonstop activities.

When emotional intensity rises or behavior becomes inconvenient, clinical language quickly enters the conversation.

In some cases, medication is introduced not because of severe psychiatric instability, but because life feels unmanageable.

We must ask tough questions:

Are we distinguishing between developmental struggle and diagnosable impairment?

Between immaturity and mental illness?

Between identity formation and psychiatric disorder?

Not every emotional struggle requires clinical intervention.

However, in the public eye, everything emotional is increasingly categorized under "mental health."

This is where the confusion begins.

Clinical mental health care was designed for treatment, stabilization, and risk management. It exists to assess impairment, diagnose disorders, reduce symptoms, and protect liability.

Insurance reimbursement requires a diagnosis.

No diagnosis means no payment.

This structure shapes how services are delivered.

Many people entering counseling are not asking for treatment of severe psychiatric illness.

They are asking:

Can someone hear me?

Can someone guide me?

Can someone help me understand who I am?

Those needs are relational.

They are not always medical.

When community programs, mentorship initiatives, and resilience-building efforts are placed in the same category as licensed clinical services, the boundary collapses.

If a program does not diagnose, does not bill insurance, and does not provide medical treatment, why is it evaluated under clinical mental health criteria?

If community grants still require clinical-style documentation, what are we truly funding: community support or clinical systems under a different name?

Are we funding:

- Crisis stabilization?

- Long-term treatment of severe impairment?

- Or relational development and identity restoration?

When everything is labeled "mental health," we lose precision.

When we lose precision, families lose clarity.

Parents do not know whether their child needs mentorship or medication.

Teenagers do not know whether they are developing or disordered.

Community leaders do not know how to differentiate their work from clinical systems.

Grant funders collapse categories because the language overlaps.

This is not an attack on clinical care.

Clinical intervention is essential for suicidality, psychosis, severe bipolar instability, debilitating trauma, and major functional impairment. Failure to treat severe illness is not reform, it is negligence.

Expanding clinical categorization into every form of normal human struggle is not reformed either.

It is drifting.

The crisis may not simply be a shortage of clinicians.

It may be a collapse of boundaries between treatment and transformation.

Until we clearly define who needs clinical care and who needs community,

we will continue to confuse stabilization with identity formation, symptom relief with resilience, and busyness with growth.

That confusion is shaping policy, funding, education, and an entire generation.

Our culture now uses therapy for:

- Self-discovery

- Weekly emotional venting

- Personal growth

- Identity exploration

There is nothing inherently wrong with wanting those things.

Human beings are wired for reflection, growth, and connection.

However, historically, clinical counseling was structured for:

- Treatment

- Stabilization

- Intervention

When did those categories blur?

When did a system designed to address severe impairment become the primary cultural space for belonging?

This is where the confusion begins.

The Warning

I have collaborated with people who have been in the mental health system their entire lives. They had seen many counselors. They carried years of clinical notes and prescriptions.

However, when they came to me, something different happened.

I approached them relationally.

I told them their emotions were normal.

I invited their partner into the conversation.

We focused on communication, self-awareness, and understanding one another.

They felt relief almost immediately.

There is a difference between relational care and clinical treatment.

It reminds me of something that happened the last time I went to the dentist.

The assistant was placing tools in my mouth, pushing them down my throat without any awareness or empathy. She had headphones on, listening to music, completely disconnected. At one point, she even placed a filling in my front tooth while it was still bleeding, leaving dried blood in the tooth.

There was no awareness.

No empathy.

No care for the fact that I was a human being sitting there.

That is what it feels like when systems lose their humanity.

Many individuals today are becoming emotionally disconnected in the same way because of early childhood neglect, lack of accountability, and the absence of vulnerability in relationships.

We must bring relationships back.

Because if we continue to call the diagnostic infrastructure "community,"

If we continue to fund categorization while neglecting belonging,

If we continue requiring impairment language before offering support,

Then we will slowly reshape how people understand themselves.

When every struggle is filtered through a clinical lens, identity and excuses become symptoms instead of a testimony.

When reimbursement requires a diagnosis, the diagnosis will expand.

When funding prioritizes stabilization over mentorship, resilience will weaken.

This is not an argument against therapy.

It is a warning against drift.

A stabilization model cannot carry the weight of identity formation.

A billing structure cannot replace belonging.

A diagnosis cannot discipline a generation.

If we fail to draw the boundary clearly, we will not merely expand treatment; we will also expand the scope of the problem.

We will redefine normal human struggle as illness.

Once that shift becomes cultural, reversing it will not be simple.

Clinical care must be protected for severe impairment.

Community must be restored for human development.

If we do not correct the confusion now,

We will build a society fluent in symptom language.

The real challenge is helping individuals desire resilience, accept responsibility, and choose growth.

The Rise of Therapeutic Culture

Something significant has shifted in the way modern society interprets human struggle.

One of the broader cultural forces shaping modern mental health systems is what sociologists describe as therapeutic culture.

Therapeutic culture refers to the growing tendency in modern societies to interpret everyday life experiences through psychological and clinical frameworks. Emotions, relationships, personal identity, and even moral decisions increasingly become framed as matters of mental health or psychological well-being rather than relational, spiritual, or developmental challenges.

Sociologist Frank Furedi describes therapeutic culture as a social shift in which emotional vulnerability becomes a central lens through which individuals interpret their experiences. In this environment, everyday struggles such as conflict, disappointment, grief, or uncertainty are often understood through the language of therapy and psychological diagnosis rather than through community support, moral guidance, or personal resilience (Furedi, 2004).

Similarly, sociologist Eva Illouz argued that therapeutic language has become deeply embedded in modern culture, shaping how people understand relationships, identity, and emotional life. Concepts originally developed within clinical psychology have expanded into education systems, workplaces, media, and everyday conversation, gradually redefining how individuals interpret normal human experience (Illouz, 2008).

This cultural shift does not mean that therapy itself is harmful. Psychological insight has helped many people understand trauma, emotional regulation, and interpersonal dynamics. However, when therapeutic frameworks become the dominant language for interpreting human experience, the boundary between normal development and psychological disorder can become blurred.

In such environments, people may begin to view ordinary struggles such as adolescence, relationship conflict, grief, or uncertainty about purpose primarily through clinical categories rather than through mentorship, community wisdom, or spiritual formation.

As therapeutic culture expands, professional mental health systems often become the primary place where individuals seek guidance about identity, relationships, and emotional struggles. However, many of these issues were historically addressed through families, elders, mentors, faith communities, and local relationships.

Understanding therapeutic culture helps explain why many people today feel confused about where to turn for help. When psychological language dominates cultural conversation, it can become difficult to distinguish between problems that require clinical treatment and challenges that require wisdom, community, and personal growth.

The issue before us is not whether therapy should exist. The deeper question is whether therapy has begun to replace the very social and spiritual structures that were designed to form resilient human beings in the first place.

I find it confusing when adults in families live in chaotic cycles of substance abuse and constant arguments. However, they send their child to be counseled while holding no accountability themselves.

What is even more confusing is when you see families still taking controlled substances that were intended for short-term use, yet they see no problem with that.

One of the most confusing realities for many people is that the individuals providing counseling are often incredibly young professionals who have spent their graduate education studying theory and clinical models but may not yet have lived through many of the experiences they are helping others navigate.

Many counselors enter the field after completing graduate degrees. However, they may not have experienced marriage, raising children, financial hardship, addiction within a family, or the long-term struggles that shape relationships over time. The degree covers psychological models, diagnostic criteria, and therapeutic techniques, but it does not automatically provide the life experiences that many clients seek guidance with.

Instead, clinicians are trained in structured approaches: reflecting on a client's statements, asking open-ended questions, closing sessions within time boundaries, and applying theoretical treatment models. These tools can be valuable and appropriate within clinical care. They are designed to create professional boundaries, protect both the client and the counselor, and ensure that treatment follows ethical and evidence-based guidelines.

For many people, this creates a deeper question.

When someone is facing the realities of marriage, family conflict, raising children, or overcoming destructive habits, they are often looking for wisdom—not just technique.

When those two forms of support are confused or replaced with one another, the result is exactly what we see today:

People search for wisdom in systems designed primarily for treatment.

Historically, guidance about life was often sought from elders, mentors, and individuals who had walked through those seasons themselves.

Scripture repeatedly emphasizes the value of wisdom passed down through generations.

In many biblical passages, counsel is associated with elders, people who have lived long enough to develop discernment through experience, hardship, and faithfulness.

This raises an important question.

Why has modern culture shifted so strongly toward professional models of counseling rather than relational wisdom passed down through the community?

Part of the answer is safety.

Clinical models provide structure. They establish ethical guidelines, protect both clients and counselors through professional standards, and create systems intended to promote accountability.

Evidence-based models are designed to reduce harm and standardize care.

Those protections matter.

When structured models become the only form of guidance available, we risk losing something equally important that grows through lived experience.

People often need both:

Professional care when there is severe impairment or crisis.

Wise mentorship is required when life requires guidance, perspective, and growth.

When those two forms of support are confused or replaced with one another, the result is exactly what we see today:

People search for wisdom in systems designed primarily for treatment.

Furthermore, that confusion continues to grow.

One of the deeper sources of confusion in modern mental health systems involves the role of professional authority and institutional power. Sociologists describe this process as medicalization: the tendency for human experiences and social problems to be increasingly interpreted and managed through medical frameworks rather than social or relational ones (Conrad, 2007).

Medicalization does not necessarily occur because professionals intend harm. Rather, it often develops when institutions that hold authority—such as medical, educational, and insurance systems—begin defining and managing more areas of human life through diagnostic categories. Over time, struggles that were once addressed through family, community, or mentorship may become reframed as clinical conditions requiring professional intervention.

This shift also creates power dynamics within systems of care. Professionals with diagnostic authority can define problems, determine treatment pathways, and control access to services. Sociologists note that when authority to define distress becomes concentrated within professional systems, the balance of power can shift away from individuals and communities and toward institutional frameworks (Foucault, 1973; Conrad, 2007).

Financial Incentives and Boundary Drift

The confusion between clinical care, community formation, education, and spiritual mentorship may not be the result of cultural drift alone. In many cases, financial structures unintentionally encourage institutions to expand beyond their original purpose.

Clinical mental health systems, for example, operate within insurance and reimbursement models that require a diagnosis for services to be covered. When funding is tied to diagnostic categories, systems may gradually begin interpreting more human struggles through clinical frameworks. This does not necessarily occur because clinicians intend harm, but because institutional structures reward diagnostic classification.

Educational institutions face similar pressures. Universities and training programs are often evaluated by enrollment numbers, graduation rates, and job placement statistics. As a result, the system tends to emphasize credential production and career pathways, sometimes at the expense of deeper formation in identity, purpose, and relational development.

Churches can experience comparable pressures when institutional survival becomes dependent on attendance numbers, program participation, or financial giving. As these pressures grow, churches may shift toward program-driven structures or entertainment-based models to maintain engagement and financial sustainability.

In sociology, these dynamics are sometimes described as institutional drift, in which organizations slowly adapt their missions to the incentives that sustain them.

Over time, these incentives can blur the boundaries between systems.

Clinical care expands into areas of human development.

Churches adopt programmatic models rather than relational discipleships.

Educational systems are producing credentials, but they're not truly helping people grow into who they're meant to be.

The result is not necessarily intentional corruption, but a gradual reshaping of institutions around the structures that fund them.

When financial incentives begin to shape institutional behavior, the original purpose of each system can slowly be distorted.

Restoring healthy boundaries, therefore, requires more than cultural awareness. It also requires recognizing how financial and structural incentives shape institutional operations.

Insurance and reimbursement structures can reinforce this pattern as well. Because many services require a diagnostic code for payment, categorization often becomes the gateway to care. Researchers have observed that this structure can unintentionally expand diagnostic labeling—not necessarily because clinicians intend to mislabel individuals, but because the system requires classification for services to be reimbursed (Conrad & Barker, 2010).

These dynamics can create confusion for families and individuals. When authority, diagnosis, and reimbursement are tightly connected, people may struggle to distinguish between normal human distress, developmental challenges, and genuine psychiatric disorders. The result is a cultural environment where professional power, institutional structures, and medical language increasingly shape how people interpret their own experiences.

Recognizing these dynamics does not mean rejecting clinical care. Severe psychiatric illness requires professional treatment and medical stabilization. However, understanding how institutional authority and diagnostic frameworks operate helps clarify why many individuals feel uncertain about where the boundaries between treatment, development, and community support truly lie.

So where do we draw the line?

Where do healthy people go for support?

When we search online for help, why are most of the available services still categorized under mental health?

Why does funding seem to focus only on job development, education, and poverty-mindset programs?

Why can't funding support relationship building, communication skills, workplace empowerment, tools for stronger marriages, celebrations that bring people together, or creativity workshops that help people build identity?

Why do we keep focusing on sickness instead of building a healthy community around what actually helps people grow?

How Billing Structures Shape the System

I know I repeated this in the research a couple of paragraphs earlier, but I would like to explain.

In many healthcare systems, insurance reimbursement requires a diagnostic code before services are reimbursed. This means clinicians must assign a recognized diagnosis to bill insurance for counseling or therapy sessions.

Because payment is tied to diagnosis, the system can unintentionally encourage situations in which human struggles are interpreted through diagnostic categories to secure reimbursement for care. Researchers studying medicalization have noted that institutional rules, such as reimbursement requirements, can influence how conditions are classified and treated.

This does not necessarily mean clinicians intend harm or mislabel people. Instead, it shows how financial structures and policy frameworks shape behavior inside institutions.

Over time, this system expands the reach of clinical care. Issues that once belonged in mentorship, family guidance, community relationships, or spiritual counsel are now pulled into clinical settings, because that's where the funding and power are.

In this sense, insurance reimbursement systems can unintentionally empower institutional responses to human problems, even when some of those problems are developmental, relational, or social rather than clinical.

Why This Matters for Boundaries

When reimbursement systems require a diagnosis for payment, clinical services become the only path to help. Meanwhile, community mentorship, relational guidance, and spiritual formation are left without real support or funding.

This imbalance can gradually shift where people go for help.

Clinical systems then carry responsibilities that historically belong to community relationships and social networks.

Recognizing these incentive structures does not mean rejecting clinical care.

Severe mental illness still requires professional treatment and stabilization.

Understanding how billing and reimbursement influence systems helps explain why the boundary between treatment and human development can become blurred.

When Systems Replace Shepherds

For most of human history, people did not first turn to institutions when they faced hardship.

They turned to people.

They turned to those who knew them, walked with them, and helped guide them through the complexities of life.

In many cultures, these individuals served as what could be described as shepherds.

Shepherds were not merely authority figures.

They were guides, mentors, elders, and spiritual leaders who walked alongside others during seasons of struggle, uncertainty, and growth.

They offered wisdom, correction, encouragement, and perspective.

A shepherd does more than manage a problem. A shepherd walks with people through it.

They listen when someone is confused.

They offer wisdom when someone is searching for direction.

They speak with hope when someone is discouraged.

They help individuals make meaning out of hardship.

Modern systems, however, were never designed to replace this role. Clinical institutions were created to stabilize severe mental illness, protect vulnerable individuals, and provide treatment during crisis. These systems serve an important and necessary function.

As therapeutic culture expanded, many of the struggles that were once navigated within communities gradually moved into institutional spaces. Questions about identity, purpose, grief, relationships, and personal direction increasingly became redirected toward professional systems.

In this transition, something subtle began to change. Systems designed to treat illness slowly began carrying responsibilities that once belonged to shepherds.

 Systems are structured to manage symptoms, document care, and follow regulated procedures. They are not designed to walk alongside people in the deeper questions of meaning, faith, and personal direction.

This creates a quiet tension within modern helping professions. Many individuals working within these systems genuinely care about the people they serve and want to offer deeper encouragement, wisdom, and guidance. Nevertheless, the policies governing their work often limit what they are permitted to say or do.

I was reminded of this tension during a conversation I once had with a man working in transportation services for individuals receiving mental health care.

His job is to transport people who are struggling with serious mental illness to appointments, hospitals, and treatment facilities.

During our conversation, he shared something that deeply struck me. He told me that many of the people he transports are hurting, confused, and searching for answers. As a man of faith, he often feels a powerful desire to talk with them about God, encourage them spiritually, and help point them toward hope and deliverance.

He said he cannot.

According to the policies governing his work and license, he is not allowed to speak about faith or spiritual guidance while performing his duties. Doing so could cost him his license and his job.

When he told me this, I remember thinking how strange that reality is. Here is a man of God spending hours deeply with people who are struggling deeply, sometimes sitting quietly with them during long rides to and from appointments, yet he cannot share the very thing he believes could bring them hope.

In many ways, it felt confusing. Transportation workers, counselors, and caregivers often spend more time with individuals in crisis than anyone else in the system. They are present in the ordinary moments, the in-between spaces where real conversations naturally happen.

The very environments where meaningful guidance could occur are often restricted by policies that separate emotional care from spiritual conversation.

This moment stayed with me because it reveals something deeper about the systems we have created. Many people within helping professions genuinely want to bring hope, wisdom, and spiritual encouragement to those they serve. Nevertheless, the structures surrounding these professions often prevent them from doing so.

The result is a strange tension: people are allowed to discuss diagnoses, medications, and symptoms, but conversations about faith, purpose, and spiritual hope are often treated as inappropriate or prohibited.

For many individuals seeking healing, however, these are the very questions they are asking.

This story reflects a larger cultural shift. Over time, systems designed to help people have slowly replaced the role that shepherds, mentors, elders, and spiritual guides once held in communities. Professional services now carry responsibilities that were historically shared among families, faith communities, and trusted relationships.

Systems are designed to manage care.

However, shepherds were meant to guide souls.

Systems can document symptoms.

Shepherds sit with people through suffering. Systems can provide treatment plans.

Shepherds help people find meaning, direction, and hope.

When systems replace shepherds, something essential is lost. The deeper human need for guidance, belonging, and spiritual direction cannot be fully met through institutional structures alone.

This is not a criticism of those working within these systems. Many people within them care deeply and want to help. Nevertheless, the structures surrounding their work often limit what they are allowed to say, what they are allowed to do, and how deeply they are allowed to engage.

As a result, many professionals quietly carry a tension between what their roles require and what their hearts believe people truly need.

The man in that vehicle was one example of this tension. Sitting with hurting individuals for hours at a time, he carried something he believed could bring hope, yet the system around him required silence.

This reveals a deeper truth: when institutions cannot speak to the deeper needs of the human spirit, communities must.

Healing has never belonged to institutions alone. It has always grown in relationships, in shared wisdom and lived knowledge, in patience, and in communities willing to persevere, building resilience and walking alongside others with understanding, presence, and unconditional love.

This concern does not leave me. Some of life's most meaningful conversations and turning points are not planned; they happen in unexpected moments: a stranger's presence, a conversation in a difficult season, or a word spoken at the right time.

For people of faith, these are not coincidences. They are divine appointments, God placing people in each other's path with purpose.

Within many modern systems, the freedom to engage in those kinds of conversations is often restricted. Policies, regulations, and professional boundaries can limit what people are allowed to say, even when the intention is simply to offer hope, encouragement, or spiritual guidance.

When systems begin regulating the very interactions where compassion, wisdom, and spiritual encouragement might naturally occur, a tension emerges. The structure designed to protect people can sometimes unintentionally prevent the kinds of human connections that have historically helped people find meaning, direction, and hope.

For many people of faith, this raises an important question: what happens when the structures designed to help people begin to limit their freedom to respond to what they believe are divine opportunities to care for others?

This tension does not mean systems are unnecessary. Systems serve important roles in providing safety, treatment, and support. However, it does raise an important reflection about the balance between institutional structure and the deep human responsibility to care for one another when the moment arises.

The question before us is not whether systems should exist. Systems serve important roles. The deeper question is whether we have allowed systems to replace the very human structures that were meant to sustain people in the first place.

If institutions cannot carry the full burden of healing, then something else must rise to meet that need.

That question leads us to the next chapter.

What kind of communities must we begin building again?

PART V

REBUILDING THE COMMUNITY

CHAPTER 11

REBUILDING THE VILLAGE

COMMUNITY OVER INSTITUTIONAL

The Vision: What a Healthy Community Looks Like. This is a hard chapter to look at because it is a mindset that takes us back to the beginning, a cycle that worked from the beginning, in a world where phones have taken over, T.V., entertainment, and the thrill of immorality. Schools are turning into confinements and institutions rather than places of enjoyment and learning.

A grade is put on identity; not all students are test takers, they learn in diverse ways. ADHD is put on individuals who have different personalities to conform to normalization, but God conformed each one individually. Individuals do not want their children outside playing because they feel it is unsafe, and they are playing video games all day.

We are made to socialize. I just took my child to a birthday party at a trampoline place; he instantly made friends, and we exchanged phone numbers with parents to allow the kids to meet up.

He was able to socialize freely and enjoyed the simple freedom of talking, playing, and being included with the other kids, something that genuinely surprised him because he never believed he would be able to. He was so happy to meet new kids and their parents. It meant even more to him when he was invited to go to other places together with the families.

We are called to stay childlike, to connect with people, exchange numbers, share ideas, and share our testimonies.

When I was there, I met several women who shared their pain of going through a divorce, being cheated on, and the grief and pain they went through, only to tell a greater story of hope and how they met a good partner who treats them right.

Stories give others hope that if God would do that for them, he would do the same for me.

What can we create for adults and teens to get out and socialize that is appealing to this group, even the elderly, and that provides a suitable place and environment to escape isolation?

Civic engagement is needed to come back,

Religious participation in discipleship, not rituals, and neighborhood interaction.

We need more clubs and local networks, not bars, but healthy places.

Over the last several decades, researchers have documented a measurable decline in civic engagement, religious participation, neighborhood interaction, and shared social life. Sociologist Robert Putnam's landmark work *Bowling Alone* demonstrated that Americans participate less in community organizations, churches, clubs, and local networks than previous generations. U.S. Surgeon General Advisory on Loneliness (2023). At the same time, national data show rising rates of anxiety, depression, and loneliness, particularly among youth, CDC Youth Risk Behavior Survey (latest trends report. These trends are related.

In recent decades, portions of Western church culture have reflected broader societal shifts toward consumerism and entertainment-driven models. Sociologist Christian Smith identified a pattern he calls *"Moralistic Therapeutic Deism,"* describing a form of faith centered more on personal comfort and feeling good than on repentance, transformation, and deep discipleship. [1] Theologian David Wells has likewise argued that modern evangelicalism has, in some contexts, lost theological depth in favor of cultural relevance and growth strategies. [2]

This does not characterize every church, and many congregations remain biblically grounded and faithful.

Cultural pressures toward marketing, expansion, and attraction-based ministry have influenced parts of the modern church landscape.

As emphasis shifts toward experience and institutional growth, accountability, repentance, and spiritual formation can become secondary.

When the community becomes performance-oriented rather than discipleship-centered, the church risks mirroring the culture rather than transforming it.

We do not need more automatic diagnosis.

We need discernment.

We do not need endless institutional expansion.

We need relational rebuilding.

We do not need more religion.

We need discipling.

In many communities today, the primary avenues for support appear to be clinical services, institutionalized education systems, or large performance-oriented religious environments.

While each serves a significant role, many individuals still report feeling unseen, unknown, and disconnected within them.

Increasingly, care, education, and ministry operate within credentialed, degree-based, and billing-driven frameworks that prioritize structure, compliance, and measurable outcomes.

Even initiatives that call themselves "community" sometimes mirror clinical or institutional models rather than relational ones.

This is not an argument against professional care, education, or church leadership; each has a necessary function.

Rather, it is a call for clarity of purpose. Clinical care stabilizes the crisis. Schools educate; churches disciple.

Community, however, is by nature different.

When every need is absorbed into formal systems, we risk overlooking the simple but powerful role of belonging, mentorship, accountability, and shared life.

Rebuilding healthy communities does not require dismantling institutions.

It requires allowing each sphere to operate within its calling and restoring relational spaces that exist before crisis, beyond billing structures, and outside performance metrics.

Research supports this distinction.

Large-scale studies show that social isolation significantly increases risk for depression and anxiety, while strong social relationships function as protective factors.

When the community weakens, emotional vulnerability increases (Holt-Lunstad et al.; PLOS Medicine, 2010). Community is not a replacement for clinical care; it is the foundation that prevents a crisis from escalating into a diagnosis.

Identity Before Intervention

In a healthy community, families talk with authority and conviction; they do not merely coexist.

Churches disciple rather than simply gather crowds.

Mentors guide with presence and investment, not just offer advice from a distance.

Elders step in to build and shape, rather than stand back and observe.

Identity is rooted in belonging, not in performance or achievement.

Clinical care has an essential role in stabilizing a crisis, but the community builds strength before a crisis ever emerges.

Diagnosis asks, "What is wrong?" while the community asks, "Who are you becoming?"

We do not need more automatic labeling; we need discernment.

We do not need endless institutional expansion; we need intentional relational rebuilding.

Identity must come before intervention.

Biblically, every person is made in the image of God; struggle does not define worth, and identity is rooted in Christ rather than in symptoms or diagnoses.

Socially and neurologically, this truth aligns with how humans are designed.

We are formed relationally, known, shaped, and strengthened within a community.

Research in social neuroscience shows that belonging regulates stress responses, supports emotional stability, and strengthens resilience, while isolation heightens anxiety and vulnerability.

Healing often begins not with labeling what is wrong, but with restoring connection and accountability in safe relationships.

In healthy communities, people are seen beyond symptom codes; their stories matter, their growth is personal, and responsibility is shared.

Community does not replace clinical care when a crisis requires stabilization, but strong relational foundations can prevent unnecessary escalation by building resilience before distress becomes disorder.

Healing happens in belonging.

Neuroscientific research demonstrates that relational connection regulates stress hormones and supports emotional resilience. Loneliness activates threat responses in the brain, while healthy attachment lowers stress and increases emotional stability (Cacioppo & Cacioppo, 2018).

Clinical care stabilizes the crisis.

Community builds strength before a crisis.

Preventive community structures historically absorbed stress before it became pathology. As those structures decline, more individuals enter clinical systems for issues that were once buffered by relational networks.

The Structural Problem We Must Solve

The current system increasingly rewards diagnosis, documentation, reimbursement, and institutional growth. These mechanisms serve administrative and regulatory purposes, but they also shape what we prioritize and how we define need.

Meanwhile, the relational infrastructure that once formed identity mentoring, parental guidance, intergenerational investment, moral formation, and shared accountability receives minimal structural support.

As civic engagement declines and loneliness rises, more individuals enter systems designed to manage crisis rather than cultivate strength. Sociological research has documented the erosion of community participation, while public health leaders now describe loneliness as an epidemic.

When every emotional struggle is immediately absorbed into the language of "mental health," the community risks being swallowed by the medical model. This is not an argument against clinical care; crisis stabilization is necessary and lifesaving. However, it is a warning.

Rising mental health statistics may not simply reflect personal fragility; they may reflect relational collapse.

When civic engagement drops, loneliness increases. When loneliness increases, anxiety and depression follow.

We are expanding institutions to manage distress, yet we are underinvesting in the relationships that prevent distress from escalating in the first place.

The question is not whether care is needed; it is whether training has been neglected.

Here is the problem clearly stated:

We have built systems that respond to breakdowns, but we have not sustained systems that build resilience.

More specifically:

1. We medicalize what was once relatively buffered.

2. We fund crisis response more than preventative formation.

3. We credential care but under-resource the community.

4. We measure pathology but rarely measure belonging.

5. We institutionalize responsibility that used to be shared socially.

In short:

We have shifted from formation-based communities to crisis-based intervention.

That is the structural issue.

Not that therapy is wrong.

Not that schools are wrong.

Not that churches are wrong.

But that: When families weaken, churches entertain rather than disciple, mentors disappear, elders withdraw, and neighborhoods disconnect, emotional strain migrates into clinical systems.

The system expands because of community contracts.

That is the structural imbalance.

The structural problem we must solve is not simply rising diagnoses, but the erosion of the relational ecosystems that once formed resilient people.

The rise in mental health diagnoses must be understood in context. Humans are relational beings. When families talk less, churches disciple less, mentors disappear, elders withdraw, and children grow up digitally connected but relationally alone, emotional distress increases. This is not a failure of individuals; it is a breakdown of shared life.

Rebuilding community is not nostalgic idealism; it is preventative mental health.

After recognizing the cultural shifts that have shaped our current systems, the question becomes clear: where do we begin? Rebuilding healthy communities and restoring human flourishing does not start with new programs or institutions.

It begins with restoring the foundations that help people understand who they are and where they belong. Before communities can be strengthened and systems improved, identity must be restored. When individuals understand their identity and anchor themselves in truth, they gain the stability needed to navigate relationships, purpose, and personal growth.

RESTORE

Identity and Truth

Before anything can be rebuilt, something must first be restored. Human flourishing begins with identity, truth, and the relationships that help anchor both.

Restore focuses on:

- Identity

- Purpose

- Personal responsibility

- Faith

- Wisdom

- Family roles

- Moral clarity

Through many of my interactions, whether shopping, driving to appointments, sitting on porch steps, meeting in homes, hotels, or restaurants, I have had countless conversations with people from every walk of life. In all those moments, one truth became truly clear to me.

People are searching for identity.

Many individuals came into my office. I stepped into their homes. Others I met in ordinary places, the marketplace, a waiting room, or in conversations that began unexpectedly.

However, in all these encounters, one thing was remarkably consistent: no one ever failed to mention God.

Sometimes it was spoken in faith.

Sometimes in confusion.

Sometimes in frustration.

Sometimes in quiet hope.

The question of God was always there.

This is why understanding Biblical identity is so important. Beneath the struggles people face, whether emotional, relational, or personal, there is often a deeper question being asked: *Who am I, and where do I belong?*

Without a clear sense of identity rooted in truth, people are left searching for meaning in a world full of conflicting voices.

However, when identity is restored, many of the questions people carry begin to find direction.

Even my atheist friends entertain their own conversations about God. Through counseling transgender and bisexual individuals, many would bring their Bibles into counseling. I have gay clients who openly talk about their relationship with God.

What this revealed to me is something deeply human: regardless of background, identity, struggle, or belief, people continue to wrestle with the question of God. Beneath the surface of many conversations is the same search for truth, belonging, and identity.

Many people do not deny God, but they deny religious organizations that communicate rituals and work against personal relationships. We forgot that the meaning of church is gathering, in grocery stores, at home, and wherever we talk about our lives, experiences, and the purpose God is calling us to.

It is when we know our identity in Christ, the one who made us, designed us, and established gifts in us, that we can become purposeful.

I went to church my whole life, but it was all over the place, trying to find out who I was. Religion never gave me my identity; if anything, it hurt me. Everything changed one day in 2005 when I met a woman who represented Christ's love at a daycare where I had taken my child.

I went home for two weeks and talked to God. I told Him that something was missing in my life, and if what I had seen was real, I wanted it.

That moment began a process of surrendering everything: the man God would choose for me, my destiny, my job, my relationships, and even the music I would listen to. God began changing my mindset and delivering me from lust and vanity.2 Corinthians 5:17 (KJV)

"If any man be in Christ, he is a new creature: old things are passed away; behold, all things are become new."

I became new with a Christ mind, no more gossip, drama, chaotic cycles, drinking, or a perverted mindset. This is when identity and purpose begin to take shape.

I have friends who do not necessarily believe in God, yet they still tell me, "For some reason, you make me believe there is a God." We do not need to force belief onto others. We simply unconditionally love people, and God will meet them in His timing.

I know people are in pain every day. Throughout my life, I have had friends who helped me through survival mode. We need to become people who are not defined by symptoms, but by testimony.

How did we get through those symptoms?

How did we get through those circumstances?

If I did, could you?

Being vulnerable about who we are helps others face their own trials and tribulations. Being honest about how we felt in those moments allows people to connect with their own emotions.

When one person opens up, it allows others to relate.

People often identify themselves by symptoms because symptoms are easy to categorize. It is easier to say, "This is my diagnosis."

Symptoms alone do not build relationships, recovery, or meaningful conversation. They do not build vulnerability, create connections, or solve human life problems.

Real redemptive stories do something different. They build vision. They give hope. They show others that transformation is possible.

Scripture is filled with these stories of redemption. Mary Magdalene was delivered from demons and became one of the first witnesses of Jesus' resurrection. The woman at the well encountered Jesus and shared her story with her town, leading many to believe in Him. Zacchaeus, a dishonest tax collector, repented and restored what he had taken from others. The apostle Paul persecuted Christians before encountering Jesus and becoming one of the greatest preachers of the gospel.

The man possessed by demons was healed and sent to tell others what God had done for him. The blind man who was healed testified simply, "Whereas I was blind, now I see."

These stories show that redemption happens when people encounter God, experience transformation, and then share their testimony so others can see God's power to change lives.

Through personal transformation, the Bible's redemption stories teach us that transformation is possible for anyone who encounters God. These stories show that people can move from brokenness, sin, or difficult circumstances into a new life through God's grace.

When someone experiences redemption, their heart, actions, and purpose begin to change. Redemption stories teach that transformation is not just about forgiveness; it also leads to a new identity, changed behavior, and a testimony that can help others find hope and change.

Through my counseling experiences, living in apartments, going to tons of churches, and meeting people in homes, I have witnessed some of the greatest redemption stories. I have seen transformation in people's lives, not overnight, but through time. I have walked alongside others who were, and still are, going through the process of change.

Before communities can change, people must rediscover who they are.

Restoring identity begins by helping individuals reconnect with truth, purpose, and belonging. For many, this identity is found in Christ. For others who may not yet believe in God, identity can still begin to be restored through the principles God established for human life: love, endurance, compassion, responsibility, and walking through suffering together.

When people support one another through hardship, listen to one another's stories, and pursue purpose together, identity begins to take shape again.

Regardless of belief, people need a sense of belonging, meaning, and direction. Communities that walk alongside individuals with patience, honesty, and care help restore identity in ways that systems alone cannot accomplish.

Restoring identity alone is not enough.

Even as individuals rediscover who they are, they still live within systems that shape how care, guidance, and human development are organized. If communities are going to truly support people in rediscovering identity and purpose, then the systems surrounding them must be examined as well.

This leads to the next step: reforming the systems and ways of thinking that shape society's response to human struggle.

Reform Systems and Thinking

Before solutions can emerge, we must first examine where our systems and cultural thinking have gone wrong.

The Loss of Parental Authority

A Cultural shift contributing to this problem is the weakening of parental authority. Modern families often face overwhelming pressures. Many parents work long hours, manage households alone, or share custody across multiple homes. During busy schedules and constant responsibilities, maintaining discipline, accountability, and consistent communication can become difficult.

In many cases, it becomes easier to outsource challenges, such as signing children up for counseling, programs, or activities, rather than address deeper family dynamics. While external support can be helpful, it cannot replace the foundational role of parents in shaping character, discipline, and identity within the home.

Schools Without Discipline

A similar shift has occurred within the education system. Schools increasingly rely on rules and policies while removing the authority structures that once reinforced discipline. When rules exist without meaningful accountability, they gradually lose their effectiveness.

Rules are meant to guide behavior, but discipline reinforces those rules by teaching responsibility, correction, and growth. Without discipline, rules become empty expectations rather than standards that shape character. Students quickly learn that rules can be ignored without consequences, which weakens respect for authority and structure.

The same dynamic can appear in homes and institutions as well.

Institutionalized Churches

Many churches have slowly shifted from discipleship to institutionalization. Instead of evangelizing and equipping believers in the full function of the five-fold ministry, many churches now operate like marketing organizations. Leadership becomes centralized in a single figure, while the broader body of believers, the hands and arms of ministry, remain underutilized.

In place of deep discipleship, churches often rely on entertainment-driven environments that appeal to people's emotions rather than cultivating spiritual maturity through the Holy Spirit. Massive buildings are constructed at great cost, yet they often sit empty most of the week, only to be filled briefly for services designed to inspire and emotionally sustain people until the following week.

However, satisfying emotional needs alone cannot replace spiritual formation. Not everyone with influence or charisma is called to shepherd people. What the church urgently needs is not more programming or more institutional training, but genuine discipleship, mentorship built through relationships.

Real discipleship happens in everyday life: sharing meals, walking through struggles together, and investing personally in one another's growth. It cannot be replaced by membership classes, scripted studies, or institutional programs.

Systems Replacing Mentorship

Across churches, workplaces, and institutions, systems are increasingly replacing mentorship. Programming people is easier than investing in them. Scripts, structured programs, and standardized processes create efficiency and control, but they rarely cultivate transformation.

In many environments, leaders rely on easily replicable systems, approved curricula, controlled messaging, and predictable cycles that maintain organizational stability.

While these systems may function efficiently, they often limit authentic dialogue, critical thinking, and spiritual discernment. In many cases, even Bible studies must follow approved formats, avoiding questions that might challenge cultural norms or expose deeper issues.

Prophetic voices, those who speak truth, confront deception, and seek God's guidance for correction—often struggle to exist in such environments.

Systems favor stability over truth. When maintaining the structure becomes more important than pursuing transformation, accountability disappears.

The same pattern appears in other professional systems. Institutions function efficiently because programs work. Large numbers of professionals are trained to follow standardized methods, clients cycle through services, and the system continues. Beneath this efficiency, there is often little depth, which can contribute to burnout, dissatisfaction, and high turnover.

In many sectors today, the church, medicine, education, and business, success increasingly depends on performance and appearance. Social media presence, networking platforms, and public image can become more important than character, wisdom, or genuine relationships.

If something looks successful, it is assumed to be working. If something feels uncomfortable or controversial, it is often avoided.

Therapy Replacing Community

Another cultural shift is the gradual replacement of community with professionalized support systems. Therapy can be a valuable tool, particularly during times of deep crisis or trauma. However, it was never meant to replace the role of community, family, mentorship, and wise counsel.

When support becomes purely transactional, meeting with someone for one hour each week to discuss symptoms, it cannot fully replicate the depth of relational guidance that comes from trusted relationships. Healthy growth often requires ongoing conversations, shared experiences, and consistent presence in one another's lives.

Without community, therapy can sometimes become a temporary relief rather than a pathway to deeper transformation. It can assist individuals through difficult seasons, but it cannot fully replace the role of family, mentors, elders, and spiritual leaders who walk alongside people through life.

Programs Without Transformation

Programs often create the appearance of progress, but they do not necessarily produce growth. Attending a class, seminar, or meeting may provide information, but information alone rarely transforms identity, habits, or character.

True growth typically emerges through relationships, mentorship, accountability, shared experiences, and meaningful responsibility.

Programs, by contrast, can be short-term and impersonal, making it easy for participants to remain disengaged while still appearing involved.

When organizations rely primarily on programs rather than relationships, transformation is often replaced by participation.

A Culture of Overdiagnosis

Modern culture has also developed a tendency to over diagnose ordinary life struggles. When individuals experience conflict, disappointment, relationship challenges, or emotional stress, the immediate response is often to seek professional diagnosis or treatment.

Many of life's challenges have historically been addressed through wisdom, mentorship, and community relationships. A trusted friend, elder, parent, pastor, or mentor often provides guidance that helps individuals grow through difficulty rather than immediately labeling the experience as a disorder.

When every struggle becomes something to diagnose, people may gradually lose the ability to develop resilience, accountability, and problem-solving skills within community relationships.

An over-diagnosis culture can unintentionally create dependence on institutions rather than encouraging personal responsibility and relational support. Over time, this weakens the natural networks that have historically helped people develop wisdom, character, and emotional strength.

The Need for Relational Restoration

Real transformation has always emerged from relationships. Parents guiding children. Elders mentoring the next generation. Leaders walking closely with those they serve. Communities sharing responsibility for one another's well-being.

Programs and systems can support these relationships, but they cannot replace them. When communities rely solely on institutional solutions, they risk losing the very relationships that cultivate the deepest and most lasting transformation.

Restoring mentorship, discipleship, and community responsibility may be one of the most important reforms needed in our cultural systems today.

Reform does not mean destroying systems. It means putting things back in their proper place.

When villages dissolve, institutions expand.

Reform means:

- Churches return to discipleship

- Community returns to mentorship

- Healthcare focuses on illness

- Families reclaim leadership

Systems have their place, but they cannot replace the village. When systems are restored to their proper role, communities can begin to reclaim what was lost. Reforming institutions alone will not rebuild healthy societies. Real change requires people to step back into relational responsibility, neighbors supporting neighbors, mentors guiding the next generation, families strengthening their roles, and communities creating spaces where individuals can grow in belonging, accountability, and purpose.

Rebuilding communities is not merely a philosophical idea; it is a practical, measurable approach to improving human well-being. Research increasingly supports what many cultures have historically practiced: strong social connections, mentorship, and community engagement significantly improve mental, emotional, and physical health outcomes. When individuals are connected to supportive networks, rates of isolation, crisis, and long-term distress decline.

This is where rebuilding begins.

Rebuild Community and Action

Using Research to Justify Community Health Programs

A growing body of research shows that strong social connections play a significant role in both physical and mental health. Community programs that strengthen relationships and reduce isolation can improve well-being and reduce healthcare costs.

Loneliness Increases Mortality Risks

An older woman called me; she was fully mentally there. She said she needed to talk to someone because she feels isolated. She has an accent, and she feels people judge her after talking to her for a while. She went on to say churches will not allow her into bible studies because she cannot and will not use technology to sign into a bible study. She continued to say that she does not even know her neighbors or anyone around her; everyone stays isolated, and she did not have that growing up. This was not a case of mental illness; this is isolation, loneliness.

Research has found that social isolation and loneliness significantly increase the risk of early death. A large meta-analysis of social relationships and mortality found that individuals with stronger social relationships had a 50% greater likelihood of survival compared to those with weaker social connections (Holt-Lunstad, Smith, & Layton, 2010).

These findings suggest that social connection functions as a major protective factor for long-term health.

Social Support Improves Mental Health

Psychological research consistently shows that strong social support networks reduce depression, anxiety, and emotional distress. Social relationships can buffer stress and help individuals cope with difficult life circumstances (Cohen & Wills, 1985). Supportive relationships also improve emotional regulation and overall psychological well-being.

Community Engagement Builds Resilience

Participation in community activities, mentorship networks, and social groups help individuals develop resilience and adaptive coping skills. Studies on human resilience show that people who maintain supportive relationships and community connections are better able to recover from adversity and trauma (Bonanno, 2004).

Community engagement provides individuals with purpose, belonging, and shared support, which strengthens long-term emotional health.

Public Health Recognition of the Problem

In 2023, the U.S. Surgeon General issued a national advisory warning that loneliness and social isolation represent a serious public health concern. The report highlighted that weak social connections are associated with increased risks for depression, cardiovascular disease, and premature mortality (U.S. Surgeon General, 2023).

Implications for Prevention

Because social connection has such a powerful influence on health, strengthening community relationships can function as a form of preventive health care.

Community programs that encourage:

- mentorship

- relationship building

- social gatherings

- collaborative learning

- shared activities

It can help reduce isolation and improve mental and physical health outcomes. When individuals experience stronger social support and community belonging, the risk of mental health crises, substance abuse, and chronic stress can decrease.

For healthcare systems and insurers, this means that investing in community connection can reduce long-term healthcare costs.

while improving the quality of life.

The Preventative Power of Community

Community has historically played a powerful role in shaping human well-being. Long before modern mental health systems existed, people developed resilience through relationships, mentorship, and shared experiences within their communities. These everyday social structures helped individuals navigate hardship, develop identity, and find purpose.

Research in psychology and public health now confirms what communities have long practiced: strong social connections protect mental and physical health. Supportive relationships reduce stress, strengthen coping skills, and provide individuals with a sense of belonging that improves long-term well-being.

Many of the practices that build resilience are simple but deeply relational. These include mentorship relationships, shared meals, community gatherings, intergenerational relationships between elders and younger generations, collaborative learning, and celebrations that bring people together.

These kinds of activities were once common features of community life. Families gathered regularly, elders shared wisdom with younger generations, and communities created spaces for celebration, learning, and cooperation. These relational environments helped individuals develop identity, responsibility, and emotional strength.

When communities provide opportunities for connection and shared purpose, they help prevent many of the conditions that later appear as mental health crises. In this way, the community itself can function as a form of preventive health, strengthening resilience long before clinical intervention becomes necessary.

Rebuilding Preventive Community Health Partnerships

One potential path toward restoring healthy community structures involves expanding partnerships between healthcare systems and local communities. In the United States, nonprofit hospitals are required to invest a portion of their resources into community health improvement through programs known as community benefit initiatives. These programs are designed to support public health, prevent illness, and improve the well-being of the communities that hospitals serve.

Preventive community partnerships could expand this model. Hospitals and healthcare systems could collaborate with community organizations to support programs that strengthen social connections and resilience. Research consistently shows that strong social support, community engagement, and meaningful relationships improve both mental and physical health outcomes.

For example, research by Holt-Lunstad and colleagues found that strong social relationships significantly reduce mortality risk and improve long-term health outcomes (Holt-Lunstad, Smith, & Layton, 2010). Similarly, the U.S. Surgeon General has warned that loneliness and social isolation are major public health concerns that affect mental and physical health and life expectancy (U.S. Surgeon General, 2023). Studies on loneliness also show that meaningful relationships and social belonging play a critical role in psychological resilience and well-being (Cacioppo & Cacioppo, 2018).

Preventive community programs could therefore include mentorship networks, social support groups, intergenerational gatherings, shared meals, community learning opportunities, and celebrations that strengthen relational bonds. Historically, these social structures were common features of community life, allowing individuals to develop a sense of identity, belonging, and purpose within supportive relational environments.

Such partnerships also raise an important policy question. If strong communities reduce loneliness, depression, and social isolation, then investing in community development may reduce long-term healthcare costs. Expanding preventive health models to include community-based programs could allow healthcare systems to invest in relational environments that protect well-being before clinical intervention becomes necessary.

In this way, the community would not replace clinical care, but it could help restore balance. Clinical mental health systems would remain focused on treating severe illness, while community partnerships would strengthen the relational foundations that help individuals remain resilient long before a crisis emerges.

The Crises Beneath the Crises

We are witnessing rising anxiety, depression, isolation, and family instability. Clinical systems are overwhelmed. Schools are strained. Churches are crowded, yet many still feel unseen.

This is not merely a mental health surge.

It is a relational deficit.

A mentorship deficit.

A belonging deficit.

A village deficit.

When relationships weaken, institutions expand to fill the gap. Nevertheless, institutions cannot replace what a village once provided.

What Disappeared

There was a time when the community naturally raised people.

I have spoken with many people who are disillusioned with institutionalized churches. Many have stepped away from megachurches that prioritize loud music and entertainment over genuine mentorship and discipleship.

Even young people have told me they remember when churches actively reached out to youth. What happened to evangelizing and saving souls?

Discipling people and mentoring them so they can grow into their purpose is essential.

When I grew up, neighborhoods functioned differently.

We ran down the streets, and neighbors watched over us. If we were bad, they took us home and told our parents. Church buses picked us up every Sunday morning.

Neighbors engaged in each other's lives.

Today, we label them "nosy neighbors" and avoid truly knowing anyone. We keep people at a distance instead of being part of their lives.

Mentorship used to happen before a crisis.

Skills were taught in kitchens and gardens. Parents were meant to be teachers to their children. Now, many families feel forced to send children to daycare and expect teachers and school systems to raise them.

Parents are working while still trying to become adults later in life. I once counseled a parent whose teenagers felt like a burden. It shocked me to realize that many parents themselves had never grown into the maturity required to raise teenagers.

There is a problem when youth lose respect for parents, teachers, and authority. Discipline and accountability have lost their place.

Church should begin at home. Accountability should begin in the home. Mentoring and education should begin in the home. How can those things begin at home when parents themselves were never modeled on these tools?

When villages dissolve, institutions expand.

We need churches to be churches.

Community to be community.

Healthcare to care for the sick.

Each has its place.

When those boundaries blur, confusion grows, and the village disappears.

I Grew Up in A Village

I did not just read about village life.

I grew up in it.

Everyone came to my house growing up. People loved being in our living room. There was no television, just people sitting and talking about life.

Many teenagers came to my house who had problems or had run away from home. My mother was always helping them. These teens were comforted with wisdom and knowledge.

I encountered this throughout my entire life.

Every morning, the kids who lived on my street came to my porch, and we would sit and talk for hours.

It was natural.

Today, people say things are different and that we cannot trust people like we used to. The truth is, we have more access to negative news than we did before. People themselves still want the same thing they always wanted.

The Living Room Rebellion

Change does not start with buildings.

We already have plenty of buildings. Many sit empty most of the week.

Change starts in living rooms.

Backyards.

Front porches.

Neighborhood circles.

I experienced this in my own neighborhood.

When I moved in twelve years ago, I was pregnant and had two young boys. My neighbors all had perfect yards, and here I came digging up my yard to put in a fence.

One neighbor panicked seeing my son near the lawnmower. Another was upset because my pool leaked into her yard. My fence caused weeds to grow into her garden.

Across the street lived a Chinese couple. On the other side was an interracial couple.

We were all vastly different.

 I chose respect.

I apologized to the neighbor pulling weeds and offered the little money I had as a single mother. Soon, we became friends, and I helped care for her mother.

The older neighbor who worried about my fence became like a grandfather to my children.

The families across the street became a community.

Yes, I was the initiator. The community usually needs someone willing to take the initiative.

Eventually, when crises happened in the neighborhood, I was the first neighbor called.

Why?

Because relationships had been formed.

Movements begin in rooms, not systems.

Small circles.

Eight to twelve people.

Mentoring.

Accountability.

Not therapy.

Not intake forms.

Not a diagnosis.

Belonging.

The Community Common Visions

Imagine communities where gardens grow in neighborhoods and families learn to cultivate food together.

Imagine greenhouses that become spaces for education, gatherings, and even wedding celebrations.

Imagine teaching kitchens where young people learn cooking, hospitality, and life skills.

Imagine church land being used for gardens and community gatherings instead of sitting empty all week.

Workshop spaces could exist in garages, barns, coffee shops, restaurants, or empty buildings.

Markets could allow families to sell handmade goods, vegetables, crafts, and small business ideas.

Celebration spaces could honor achievements—such as GED completions, employment milestones, or personal victories. Many people never celebrated growing up. Celebration encourages people to continue their race in life.

These are the spaces where mentorship grows naturally.

This is what prevention looks like when it has land and community.

Communities Once Functioned This Way

The vision of community life described here is realistic. In many parts of history, communities functioned in similar ways.

Early Christian communities often gathered in homes rather than large institutional buildings. The book of Acts describes believers sharing meals, supporting one another, and meeting regularly for teaching, prayer, and fellowship (Acts 2:42–47). These gatherings were deeply relational. Faith, mentorship, and daily life were intricately connected.

In early Christian communities, older believers often guided younger ones in matters of faith and life. Wisdom was passed down through discipleship, shared experience, and personal relationships.

This pattern was evident in early villages and towns throughout history. Communities relied on neighbors helping neighbors, and skills were passed down through apprenticeship, where experienced individuals trained younger generations in trades, crafts, and life skills.

Local markets gave families the opportunity to sell what they produced: food, crafts, and handmade goods. Community gatherings and celebrations brought people together, strengthening relationships and honoring life's milestones.

These environments created natural mentorship networks.

People learned from elders, shared responsibility, and supported one another through both hardship and success.

Over time, many of these relational structures weakened as societies became more institutionalized and centralized.

Schools, workplaces, healthcare systems, and other institutions began carrying responsibilities that communities once shared together.

While institutions can provide important services, they cannot fully replace the relational environments that once helped people develop a sense of identity, purpose, and belonging.

Rebuilding community spaces does not require abandoning modern systems.

It simply means restoring the relational environments where people can learn, grow, and support one another.

The village may feel distant today, but it is possible to rebuild. It begins when communities choose to gather again.

Guardrails For Integrity

Movements collapse without structure.

Mentors should have testimony. Before someone leads others, they should understand why they feel called to serve.

School never taught me how to be a counselor. It taught theories and discipline. What shaped me most were the mentors who walked beside me.

Many people who struggle through something can help others overcome the same struggle. I have a friend who told me she was a pilot on an airplane.

When COVID came, they wanted her to get the vaccine, but she refused. The airline had a tough time letting her retire. They said to her, "We get a lot of customer complaints with the young girls, and we would like you, because you are older, to stay and mentor the younger women."

That stuck with me.

Many times, I love the elders because they teach me so much wisdom and knowledge. I love people in general who can say, "I have been through that." I think, wow, you have been through cancer. You will be the first person I talk to if I ever go through it.

Why would I want a mental health counselor who has never experienced certain life experiences?

Why wouldn't I want someone who has experienced a cheating husband, divorce, or someone who has experienced death and grief? If they got through it, I want to know how they survived it.

Testimony teaches survival.

Many people in the Bible were mentored before becoming leaders by the very people who had experienced things themselves.

Moses mentored Joshua before he ever led the people.

Elijah mentored Elisha before passing on leadership.

Paul mentored Timothy and trained him in ministry.

Even the disciples walked with Jesus before they ever led the early church.

Leadership in the Bible was not built on degrees.

It was built on discipleship, mentorship, and testimony.

The Bible even clearly teaches this pattern. In Titus 2, older men and older women are instructed to teach and guide the younger generation in living wisely and faithfully. Wisdom was meant to be passed down through life experience, character, and example, not solely through institutions.

The book of Proverbs also emphasizes the value of wise counsel and mentorship. Proverbs teach that wisdom grows through guidance and shared experience.

Proverbs 11:14 says:

"Where no counsel is, the people fall: but in the multitude of counselors there is safety."

Proverbs 27:17 reminds us:

"Iron sharpeneth iron; so, a man sharpeneth the countenance of his friend."

These scriptures show that growth was always meant to happen in relationships, through people sharpening and strengthening one another.

We do not need degrees to build community.

It does not take a degree to figure out life.

It takes testimony.

These are the people we should look for.

What areas are you good at?

What areas have you overcome?

How long have you been part of this community?

Those are the people who can guide others.

A single mother who survived hardship can mentor another young mother. Someone who earned a GED later in life can help another student believe it is possible.

Many things I once thought of where failures are now the very lessons I use to help others.

But boundaries matter.

Severe cases should be referred to licensed professionals. Clinical care has its place and should be honored.

The community must know when to help and when to refer.

Freedom without guardrails becomes chaos.

Guardrails without relationships become control. We build both.

A Table at The Trampoline Park

I once took my son to a trampoline park for a birthday party. My son made a new friend, so I introduced myself to the father, and we exchanged phone numbers.

The next week, his mother invited us to her son's birthday party.

We ended up sitting at a table talking for over an hour. Four other mothers joined the conversation.

We talked about God, church, relationships, and life struggles.

One Hispanic woman said that where she grew up, neighbors woke up every morning and invited each other over. When she moved to Ohio, she noticed people no longer lived like that.

Another woman shared how God transformed her character and made her a better wife. Her sister also shared her testimony.

One woman was single at forty-seven and had focused on her career. Another family, including an ex-husband, attended the party with his fiancée, and everyone treated each other with respect.

Children who were not part of the party came over and shared cupcakes and snacks.

By the time I left, I realized something.

This was what many people are searching for when they go to therapy.

A place to talk.

A place to belong.

A place where their story matters.

Biblical And Community Perspective

Scripture reminds us of a simple truth.

You are made in the image of God.

Struggle does not define you.

Identity is rooted in Christ.

Community reinforces that identity by surrounding individuals with relationships that remind them who they are.

Biblical truth restores identity.

Community surrounds the person.

The Bigger Picture

Symptom-based medicine asks:

"How do we reduce or manage this condition?"

Resilience development asks:

"How do we grow stronger through this experience?"

Both have value, but resilience builds the strength needed for life.

Resilience builds endurance.

Fortitude builds courage.

Perseverance keeps us moving forward.

Community builds these strengths over time.

The Call

Institutionalization and the Loss of Human Connection

Many sociologists have warned that as societies grow more complex, human systems often become increasingly bureaucratic and institutionalized. Bureaucracy can help organizations function efficiently, but when systems become too rigid, they can unintentionally strip away the relational elements that make communities healthy.

Sociologist Max Weber, one of the founders of modern sociology, warned that modern institutions could create what he called an *"iron cage"* of bureaucracy.

In these systems, rules, procedures, credentials, and administrative structures begin to dominate decision-making, often leaving little room for human judgment, relationships, or individual potential (Weber, 1922).

Over time, people may begin to feel that they are simply moving through systems rather than being truly seen within them.

In bureaucratic environments, individuals are often evaluated through measurable categories, grades in schools, diagnostic labels in clinical systems, productivity metrics in workplaces, or attendance numbers in institutions. While measurement can serve useful purposes, it can also reduce complex human lives into simplified categories.

When systems become overly focused on measurable outcomes, relational life can weaken.

Mentorship becomes less common.

Personal guidance becomes replaced by standardized procedures.

Human interaction becomes filtered through institutional processes.

Sociologists studying modern institutions have described this as a form of depersonalization, where individuals are treated more as cases, records, or data points rather than as whole people with stories, potential, and relationships.

This pattern can appear across many different sectors of society. In education, students may be defined primarily by grades or test scores. In workplaces, employees may be evaluated through productivity metrics and performance rankings. In clinical systems, individuals may be understood primarily through diagnostic categories. Even in religious institutions, participation may sometimes be measured through attendance, programs, or organizational growth.

When systems prioritize structure over relationships, they may become efficient, but they risk losing the human connection that allows individuals and communities to flourish.

This does not mean institutions themselves are harmful. Systems can provide structure, stability, and organization. However, when systems expand beyond their proper role and begin replacing relationships, mentorship, and community life, the balance between structure and humanity can be lost.

Healthy societies require both structure and relationships.

Institutions can provide organization and support, but human growth happens through relationships, through mentorship, accountability, shared experience, and meaningful connection.

Reform, therefore, does not require destroying systems. It requires restoring the human relationships that systems were originally meant to support.

When communities restore mentorship, discipleship, accountability, and relational life, institutions can return to their proper role, serving people rather than replacing the relationships people need to thrive.

We live in a time when systems have expanded, but relationships have weakened.

Schools educate, but often fail to form identity.

Workplaces employ people but rarely cultivate a sense of belonging. Clinical systems treat symptoms but cannot replace the community.

Churches gather crowds but sometimes struggle to discipline believers.

The problem is not that these systems exist.

The problem is that many of them have slowly taken on responsibilities they were never meant to carry.

Families were meant to form identity.

Communities were meant to build belonging.

Mentors were meant to guide the next generation.

Churches were meant to disciple believers.

When these structures weaken, institutions expand to fill the gap.

Institutions cannot replace the relational foundations that once shaped strong individuals and healthy communities.

The call before us is not simply to improve our systems.

The call is to restore what was lost.

To restore mentorship.

To restore discipleship.

To restore families that teach responsibility and love.

To restore communities where people know one another and carry one another's burdens.

This work does not begin with governments or large institutions.

It begins with people.

With living rooms opening again.

With neighbors learning each other's names.

With mentors guiding younger generations.

With churches returning to discipleship.

With communities rebuilding the spaces where belonging is formed.

The village will not rebuild itself.

Nevertheless, it can be rebuilt.

One relationship at a time.

Movements require invitation.

Do not wait for permission.

Start where you are.

Open your living room.

Mentor one youth.

Host one gathering.

Plant one garden.

Teach one skill.

Community begins with small steps.

Research Supporting Community-Based Prevention

In a perfect Community, it would be ideal for Community-based prevention.

A growing body of research shows that strong communities and social connections play a significant role in both physical and mental health. Public health researchers increasingly recognize that many human struggles are influenced not only by medical factors but also by social environments such as relationships, community participation, and access to supportive networks.

One emerging model in healthcare is known as social prescribing. In this approach, doctors and healthcare providers connect patients with community activities rather than relying solely on clinical treatment.

These referrals can include group activities such as gardening programs, walking groups, art classes, volunteer work, and social clubs. The goal is to address loneliness, stress, and other social factors that influence health.

Research shows that these community-based interventions can improve well-being by helping individuals build relationships, find purpose, and develop social support networks. Social prescribing programs aim to connect individuals with activities, groups, and services in their communities that support emotional and social needs affecting health.

Community environments themselves can also contribute to improved health outcomes. Studies examining community gardens have found that participants often experience higher levels of life satisfaction, happiness, and mental well-being than individuals who are not involved in community gardening. These environments also strengthen social cohesion and encourage relationships between neighbors.

Gardening programs have also been shown to reduce loneliness and provide opportunities for meaningful social interaction. Research suggests that community gardens create relaxed spaces where people connect with others while working together, thereby improving mental health and strengthening community bonds.

More broadly, studies on social relationships show that human connection is one of the strongest predictors of long-term health. Strong social ties are associated with improved mood, reduced stress, and even lower mortality risk. Researchers have described social connection as a major protective factor for both physical and psychological health.

These findings support an important idea: communities themselves can function as a form of preventive health care. When people have access to relationships, mentorship, shared activities, and supportive environments, many forms of distress can be reduced before they develop into serious health problems.

Community spaces such as gardens, workshops, shared meals, mentorship gatherings, and celebrations can therefore play a powerful role in strengthening both individual well-being and community resilience.

The Declaration

Clinical care stabilizes the crisis.

Community builds character.

Institutions manage breakdowns.

Villages build resilience.

Labels describe symptoms.

Belonging shapes identity.

We do not abandon systems.

We rebuild what systems cannot replace.

The next generation does not need more programs.

It needs people.

It needs land.

It needs skill.

It needs celebration.

It needs a village.

The Village Reform Manifesto

Expanding Choice in Preventive Support

Another reform would be to give individuals greater freedom to choose the type of support that best meets their needs. Currently, many insurance and healthcare systems primarily reimburse clinical mental health services. Because of this structure, individuals seeking help are often directed toward licensed clinical counseling even when their needs may involve social connection, mentorship, or community engagement rather than treatment for mental illness.

A preventive approach could allow individuals to choose how to allocate a portion of their health support resources. For example, people might have the option to use funding for clinical mental health counseling when they are experiencing severe distress or psychiatric symptoms. However, if individuals are primarily seeking social connection, personal development, mentorship, or community belonging, they could instead choose to participate in approved community programs.

These programs could include mentorship networks, community learning groups, social support gatherings, intergenerational activities, or relationship-building initiatives. Research consistently shows that strong social connections improve mental and physical health outcomes and reduce loneliness, depression, and social isolation (Holt-Lunstad, Smith, & Layton, 2010; Cacioppo & Cacioppo, 2018; U.S. Surgeon General, 2023).

Providing individuals with the ability to choose between clinical services and community-based programs could help restore balance between treatment and prevention. Clinical mental health systems would remain focused on treating severe illness, while community environments could support identity formation, belonging, and resilience.

Such a model would recognize an important truth: not every human struggle requires clinical treatment, but every person benefits from meaningful relationships and supportive community.

Research Supporting "Expanding Choice in Preventive Support"

Social Prescribing (Healthcare Referring to Community) One growing approach in healthcare is called social prescribing. Instead of prescribing medication or therapy alone, healthcare providers refer patients to community programs that address loneliness, stress, and lifestyle needs.

These programs can include:

- community groups

- volunteering

- mentorship programs

- exercise groups

- art or skill workshops

- social clubs

The goal is to address the social causes of distress, not just the symptoms.

Research shows that social prescribing can reduce healthcare visits, improve mental well-being, and increase life satisfaction.

Preventative Health Models

Public health research increasingly recognizes that preventing illness is often more effective than treating illness only after it develops. Preventive health focuses on strengthening the social and environmental conditions that support human well-being before a crisis occurs.

Preventive health approaches commonly include:

- community support networks

- lifestyle education

- social engagement

- mentorship and peer support

These factors strengthen resilience and reduce the likelihood that emotional distress develops into more serious mental health disorders (World Health Organization, 2004).

Community Health Workers

Another evidence-based model is the use of community health workers. These are trained individuals who help people:

- navigate healthcare systems

- connect to community resources

- access support services

- build social networks

Research shows that community health workers can improve health outcomes while also reducing healthcare costs by helping individuals access support before problems escalate (Viswanathan et al., 2010).

Loneliness as a Public Health Risk

Loneliness has increasingly been recognized as a significant public health concern. In 2023, the U.S. Surgeon General issued a national advisory warning that chronic loneliness and social isolation are associated with increased risks of:

- depression

- anxiety

- heart disease

- stroke

- premature death

At the same time, strong social relationships function as a powerful protective factor for both physical and mental health (U.S. Surgeon General, 2023).

Social Connection Improves Survival

One of the most widely cited studies in this field found that individuals with strong social relationships have about a 50% greater likelihood of survival compared to those with weaker social connections (Holt-Lunstad, Smith, & Layton, 2010).

Researchers note that the health benefits of social connection are comparable to major lifestyle factors such as:

- quitting smoking

- improving diet

- increasing physical activity

These findings highlight the powerful role that relationships and community support play in protecting long-term health.

Returning the Church to Discipleship

Many people today are deeply frustrated with the modern church experience. They are not rejecting faith or rejecting God. Instead, they are expressing concern that many churches no longer resemble the community model described in Scripture.

In many places, church gatherings have shifted toward entertainment-driven experiences rather than discipleship and spiritual formation. Large productions, concerts, and programs can draw crowds, but they do not necessarily cultivate repentance, accountability, mentorship, and spiritual maturity.

For many believers, the concern is not simply about style. It is about structure and purpose.

The early church described in the book of Acts was not centered around performance or entertainment. It was built around teaching, fellowship, discipleship, prayer, and shared responsibility within the body of believers (Acts 2:42–47).

Many Christians today are asking difficult but important questions:

Where is repentance being taught?

Where is spiritual accountability?

Where is mentorship between older believers and younger believers?

Where is the space for elders to guide with wisdom?

Where is the role of prophets, apostles, and spiritual leadership described in Scripture?

These concerns reflect a desire to see the church return to a biblical model of discipleship, rather than functioning primarily as a religious institution or an entertainment environment.

Research within the sociology of religion supports many of these concerns. Sociologist Christian Smith identified a widespread pattern within modern American Christianity that he calls "Moralistic Therapeutic Deism," in which faith becomes centered on personal comfort and feeling good rather than repentance, transformation, and discipleship (Smith & Denton; *Soul Searching*, 2005). This shift can unintentionally reshape churches into environments that are more focused on emotional experience than on spiritual formation.

Theologian David Wells similarly argues that portions of modern evangelical culture have gradually replaced theological depth and moral authority with marketing strategies, cultural relevance, and growth-driven programming (Wells, *No Place for Truth*, 1993; *God in the Wasteland*, 1994).

Another growing concern involves the relationship between the ministry and institutional structure. When churches begin to operate primarily as large organizations focused on programming, attendance numbers, or financial sustainability, their mission can gradually shift away from spiritual formation.

Some critics argue that when churches operate primarily as institutional organizations, questions about tax exemption and public accountability naturally arise. If churches function primarily as institutions rather than as spiritual communities devoted to discipleship, many believe they should be willing to examine whether their structures reflect their mission.

These conversations are not about weakening the church. They are about strengthening it.

Many believers are not asking for bigger buildings or more programs. They are asking for deeper discipleship.

They want repentance to be taught.

They want accountability to be practiced.

They want elders to mentor younger believers.

They want spiritual gifts and leadership roles described in Scripture to be recognized and practiced.

They want churches that look more like the community described in the book of Acts.

The church was never meant to be a concert, a program schedule, or a performance. It was meant to be a community of believers who teach truth, disciple one another, hold each other accountable, and grow together in faith.

Many believers today are not rejecting Jesus or the power of God. In fact, many are leaving institutional religious environments precisely because they believe something essential has been lost. Religion without transformation can leave people feeling powerless, discouraged, and spiritually wounded.

When faith becomes reduced to rituals, programs, or emotional experiences without true discipleship, repentance, and spiritual authority, it can create environments where people attend services but never experience the life-changing power of Christ.

The New Testament reveals a faith that transforms lives, renews minds, and breaks spiritual strongholds. The Apostle Paul spoke out against forms of religion that maintain outward appearances while denying the power of God at work within them (2 Timothy 3:5).

Biblical discipleship was never meant to produce passive followers or spectators. It was meant to form believers who are transformed through repentance, renewed thinking, and the power of the Holy Spirit.

If strongholds are not being broken, people are not being saved, and minds are not being renewed, then more buildings, prayer rooms that only appeal to the soul, or more programs will not deliver people from demons, sickness, or sin, nor will they disciple them.

True transformation requires repentance, truth, discipleship, and the renewing of the mind (Romans 12:2; 2 Corinthians 10:4–5).

Scripture consistently shows that transformation comes through the power of God working through truth, repentance, discipleship, and the renewing of the mind. Emotional experiences alone cannot break spiritual strongholds or produce lasting spiritual maturity.

The Decline of Church Effectiveness

Long-term research shows that while many people still identify as Christian, deep commitment and discipleship behaviors have declined.

A 25-year analysis by the Barna Group found that:

- Practicing Christians dropped from 46% of U.S. adults to 24%.

- The percentage of Christians who say faith is central to their life fell by about twenty percentage points since 2000.

Researchers note that when the importance of faith declines, practices like discipleship, evangelism, and church involvement also decline.

This suggests that many churches may still gather crowds but are producing fewer deeply committed disciples.

Evidence of Discipleship Deficit

Recent research examining spiritual growth among church members shows that many churches struggle to form mature disciples.

A national discipleship study found that:

- Churchgoers scored sixty-eight out of one hundred on average in spiritual development.

- Only 8% of pastors strongly agreed their church was effectively developing disciples.

Researchers have described this as a "discipleship deficit" in modern church life.

Declining In Church Participation

Large sociological studies show a long-term decline in church participation across Western countries.

For example:

- Surveys show fewer people identifying as Christian and fewer attending church regularly.

- Many denominations have experienced membership decline over recent decades.

- Church attendance in several countries has steadily dropped with the congregation's age.

These trends suggest that institutional churches often struggle to maintain engagement, especially among younger generations.

Younger Generations Are Disengaging

Studies on young people show significant disengagement from traditional church participation.

One large study found:

- Forty-five percent of Gen Z rarely or never attend church.

- Only about 1 in 4 attends regularly.

Researchers studying youth participation have found that many young people feel:

- disconnected from church leadership

- uninvolved in decision-making

- unable to relate to the teaching style or structure of services.

What Scholars Say the Problem Is

Researchers studying religion often point to several structural issues:

Institutionalization

Churches can become structured around:

- programs

- organizational growth

- attendance numbers

instead of relational discipleship.

Weak Mentorship

Studies show that intergenerational mentorship and personal discipleship are some of the strongest predictors of lasting faith.

Cultural Adaptation

Some scholars argue that churches adapt to entertainment culture, which may increase attendance but does not necessarily produce deep spiritual formation.

What The Early Church Looked Like

Biblical and historical descriptions of early Christianity show a different structure:

Acts 2:42–47 describes believers who:

- devoted themselves to teaching.

- shared meals

- prayed together

- shared resources

- met frequently in homes

Many historians note that early Christian communities were relational networks rather than large institutions.

Reform does not mean abandoning the church.

It means returning to the purpose for which it was created.

Redefining the Care System

If we are serious about reform, we must begin by defining the lines between three diverse kinds of needs:

- clinical mental illness

Normal human struggles that require community

- spiritual formation and guidance

Right now, those lines are blurred.

People enter schools, doctors' offices, counseling centers, and churches with quite diverse needs, but too often they are all directed into the same system. When everything is labeled mental health, we begin treating normal human experiences as medical problems.

We need to define the lines.

If a person walks into a doctor's office, a counseling center, school system, or even a church and says, "I feel isolated. I have no one to talk to, which already tells us something important.

That may not be mental illness.

That may be a lack of community.

When someone lacks identity, belonging, relationships, mentorship, or purpose, the solution may not be medication or long-term clinical treatment. It may be a connection. It may be guidance. It may be a community.

Doctors, mental health providers, schools, and churches need education on recognizing these differences.

When physicians prescribe medication or refer someone to a clinical mental health provider, they should be able to explain why that level of treatment is necessary. They should also be able to recognize when someone's symptoms are rooted in normal human struggles rather than psychiatric illness.

For example, anxiety that comes from fear, stress, life transitions, or isolation can be a normal human response.

Community support, mentorship, guidance, and social connection may be the appropriate response rather than immediately moving toward long-term medication.

When clinical mental health professionals diagnose someone with a mental health disorder, they should also provide clear education to patients and families. Families should understand what the diagnosis means, what the treatment plan involves, and whether medications are intended for short-term stabilization or long-term use. They should also understand how long-term dependency on medication can affect the individual and the family environment.

At the same time, the community must be acknowledged as a legitimate part of support. Community mentors can guide individuals toward resources, events, social opportunities, churches, and environments where people can develop identity, relationships, and purpose. These mentors can help people reconnect to the social and relational structures that historically helped individuals navigate life struggles.

The community needs to be visible.

Doctors, counselors, and schools should know where these community resources exist and how to refer people to them when clinical treatment is not the primary need.

One reform would be to establish regular collaborative meetings among healthcare providers, counselors, community organizations, insurance systems, and faith leaders. These gatherings could create ongoing education about the differences between clinical mental illness, community needs, and spiritual guidance.

Doctors, counselors, insurance providers, community leaders, and pastoral counselors could meet regularly to discuss how to better direct people to the type of help they need.

Right now, too many people who need identity, belonging, and social connection end up in systems designed to treat illness.

When healthy people with normal human needs remain in clinical systems for extended periods, those systems can unintentionally harm them by reinforcing the idea that something is wrong with them, when what they need is connection, purpose, and guidance.

Clinical mental health systems should focus on treating real illness.

Community should focus on belonging, mentorship, and identity.

Churches should focus on spiritual formation and discipleship.

Each system has a significant role, but those roles must be clearly defined.

Another important reform involves restoring the broader meaning of counseling. Historically, the word "counselor" referred to a person who offered wisdom, mentorship, and guidance. Today, the world is increasingly associated with licensed clinical mental health professionals.

Pastoral counseling, mentorship, and community guidance should again be recognized as legitimate forms of support that exist alongside clinical mental health treatment.

Restoring this distinction helps protect both systems.

Clinical mental health professionals can focus on treating illness.

Communities can focus on belonging.

Churches can focus on discipleship.

Not every human struggle is a mental illness.

Some people need medicine.

Some people need mentorship.

Some people need community.

Some people need spiritual guidance.

A healthy society must recognize the difference.

Reforming the Family and Community Structure

Reforming our systems must also include restoring the health of families and communities. Many families today are struggling not because they lack programs, but because they lack guidance, mentorship, and education about how to build healthy relationships. The community should help teach families how to respect one another.

Too often, family systems fall into patterns of control, competition, and emotional distance.

Instead of reinforcing dominance or elevating individual success, communities should teach respect, service, patience, and unconditional love.

Families should be equipped to listen to one another, resolve conflict, and build homes where love and accountability coexist.

Healthy families are not built through control. They are built through respect, humility, and a willingness to serve one another.

Community can also help restore knowledge about health and nutrition. Many people today only understand food through the lens of standardized food groups or industrialized food systems. Families should be educated about where food comes from, how food is grown, and the difference between organic and chemically treated foods.

Communities can teach people how food is farmed, how soil health affects human health, and how herbs and natural foods have historically been used to support the body.

Understanding what we put into our bodies is essential to human well-being. When families learn about nutrition, natural foods, herbs, and the benefits of healthy living, they gain the knowledge needed to care for their bodies and their children.

Community Shapes How Families Value Time Together

Modern culture often defines family time through busy schedules, sports practices, television, entertainment, and constant activity. While these activities can be enjoyable, they are not the same as a meaningful connection. Families need spaces where they can slow down, share meals, talk about life, pray together, and build genuine relationships.

True family time is not simply being in the same room while everyone is distracted by screens or schedules.

It is the intentional act of being present with one another.

Another important reform involves shifting families away from a culture that emphasizes individual success above everything else. Healthy families are built when members learn to serve one another rather than compete.

Service builds humility.

Service builds love.

Service builds unity.

When communities begin teaching these values again, families can rediscover the strength that comes from mutual care and responsibility.

Education also plays a critical role in reform.

Many families believe their only options for education, employment, and economic stability come through rigid institutional pathways. Nevertheless, when people are educated about the broader range of possibilities available to them, such as entrepreneurship, skilled trades, agricultural work, homeschooling, cooperative education models, and community-based learning, they begin to realize they have more options than they previously believed.

Communities can help families understand that they are not limited to one narrow system. Families can grow food. They can build small businesses. They can create local economies. They can educate their children in ways that align with their values and goals.

When people only see one path forward, they often develop mental barriers that make alternative possibilities invisible. However, when communities educate people about different ways of living, working, and raising families, those barriers begin to break down.

Community Knowledge and Natural Health

Another area where communities can rediscover wisdom is in understanding natural health and nutrition. Many people today only learn about vitamins, supplements, and medicine through the modern healthcare system. Physicians often recommend standardized pharmaceutical treatments or the most commonly available forms of supplements because they are regulated, widely studied, and easily distributed through insurance systems.

However, throughout history, communities also relied on natural knowledge about food, herbs, and plant-based remedies to support health and prevent illness.

Many traditional cultures grew herbs, prepared natural foods, and passed down knowledge about how plants could support the body.

Today, much of this knowledge has been lost or disconnected from everyday life. Many people are unfamiliar with where their food comes from, how herbs were historically used, or how nutrition supports the body's natural systems.

This does not mean modern medicine is unnecessary. Clinical medicine saves lives and plays an essential role in serious illness or medical emergencies. However, communities can complement modern healthcare by rediscovering the basic practices that support everyday health.

Community gardens, teaching kitchens, and local education programs can help families learn to grow food, prepare healthy meals, and understand the natural plant resources that have historically supported well-being. Churches and community spaces can become places where people learn about nutrition, stewardship of the body, and responsible health care.

The Bible itself references many plants, herbs, and foods used for healing and nourishment. While spiritual and medical interpretations differ, these passages remind us that caring for the body and the land has long been part of human life.

When communities reconnect with food, land, and shared knowledge, they strengthen both physical health and social relationships.

These practices are not a replacement for medical care, but they can support healthier lifestyles and reduce some of the conditions that lead to illness in the first place.

Awareness Creates Freedom

When people understand their options in nutrition, community support, education, and economic opportunities, they are less likely to blindly follow systems. Instead, they begin making thoughtful decisions about how they want to live and what kind of future they want to build for their families.

Strong communities do not simply provide programs.

They cultivate wisdom.

They teach families how to care for one another.

They teach people how to live healthy lives.

They help individuals discover purpose, responsibility, and possibility.

When communities become places of learning, mentorship, and shared responsibility, people no longer feel trapped within systems that do not serve them.

Instead, they begin building something better.

Reclaiming The Meaning of Counselor

Another important reform that must be addressed is the meaning of the word counselor itself.

For most of human history, a counselor was not defined by a license, a diagnosis, or a billing code. A counselor was someone who provided wisdom, guidance, mentorship, and direction in life.

Counselors were elders, spiritual leaders, parents, teachers, and experienced individuals who had walked through life and could help guide others.

In Scripture, the idea of counsel appears throughout the Bible. Wisdom literature repeatedly describes the importance of receiving wise counsel.

Proverbs teach:

"Where there is no counsel, the people fall: but in the multitude of counselors there is safety." (Proverbs 11:14)

Counsel in this context did not refer to a clinical diagnosis. It referred to wisdom shared within a community.

The Bible even describes Christ as the ultimate Counselor.

"And his name shall be called Wonderful, Counselor, The mighty God, The everlasting Father, The Prince of Peace." (Isaiah 9:6)

In biblical understanding, a counselor is someone who helps guide others toward truth, wisdom, and transformation.

In modern society, the word counselor has been entirely absorbed into the clinical mental health system. Today, the title "counselor" is most associated with licensed clinical professionals who operate within diagnostic frameworks and medical billing systems.

In the twentieth century, counseling became professionalized. Regulatory boards and licensing requirements reshaped the role. The modern clinical counselor is trained to diagnose mental disorders, follow ethical codes that restrict value imposition, and document treatment according to standardized psychological models.

This shift reflects a broader change. Sociologists call it the medicalization of human problems, where struggles once addressed through mentorship, family guidance, and community relationships are now redefined as conditions requiring professional intervention (Conrad, 2007).

While clinical mental health care is essential for severe psychiatric illness, the expansion of diagnostic systems has unintentionally absorbed roles that were historically fulfilled within communities.

Mentorship became therapy.

Guidance became diagnosis.

Wisdom became treatment planning.

In the process, the broader meaning of the counselor was lost.

Communities need counselors who listen to stories, share wisdom, mentor the younger generation, and help people find identity and purpose. These roles do not require clinical licenses. They require experience, integrity, discernment, and relational investment.

Reforming our systems means recognizing that clinical mental health care and community counseling serve different purposes.

Clinical counselors stabilize serious mental illness.

Community counselors' mentors guide and build resilience before a crisis emerges.

Both roles have value, but they are not the same thing.

If communities are going to be rebuilt, we must reclaim the broader meaning of counsel.

The next generation does not only need professionals.

It needs mentors.

It needs elders.

It needs wise voices who have walked through life and can say:

"I have been where you are. Let me walk with you."

The word counselor should not belong to institutions alone.

It belongs to communities.

If the village no longer exists, we will rebuild it.

In living rooms.

In gardens.

Around bonfires.

In kitchens.

In markets.

In conversations.

Through mentorship.

Through accountability.

Through shared stories.

The village is not gone.

It is waiting to be rebuilt.

The time has come to restore, reform, and rebuild it.

Where The Village Begins

When I look back at my life, I realize something simple.

The moments that shaped me most were not programs, offices, or institutions.

There were conversations on porches.

Teenagers were sitting in my living room, asking for guidance. Neighbors were learning to respect each other, even when we started with disagreements.

Mothers shared their stories around a table at a trampoline park while children played nearby.

Those moments were not planned systems.

They were people choosing to care about one another.

That is what a village looks like.

A village is not a building.

It is not a program.

It is not a diagnosis.

A village is people who decide that no one around them will struggle alone.

I have seen what happens when people feel forgotten.

I have also seen what happens when someone simply listens, mentors, or opens their door.

People begin to believe again.

Families begin to stabilize.

Young people begin to find direction.

Hope returns.

This book is not a solution to every problem our society faces. It is an invitation.

An invitation to remember that communities were never meant to function through institutions alone.

They were meant to function through people.

Through neighbors who care.

Through mentors who guide.

Through families who take responsibility.

Through communities that celebrate growth and endure hardship together.

The village may feel lost in many places today.

It is not gone.

It lives wherever someone chooses to care for the people around them. That is where rebuilding begins. The village is not something we wait for.

It is something we build.

The Village Restoration Model Summarized

Rebuilding the village requires reforming both our communities and our systems so that people once again have access to identity, mentorship, prevention, and belonging. A restored village creates environments in which individuals and families are strengthened before a crisis occurs and in which institutions return to their proper roles. A healthy community does not tolerate delays where immediacy is needed. It closes the gap.

Priority 1: Immediate Relational Access

One of the most critical elements missing from modern systems is timing.

Many individuals seek help in the middle of a crisis. They are not coming in calmly or casually. They are grieving, overwhelmed, or facing relational breakdowns that feel urgent and destabilizing.

Yet even in those moments, they are often placed into a process that requires waiting.

They must complete assessments.

They must schedule appointments.

They must enter structured systems before receiving meaningful support.

Some are told to wait days.

Others are told to wait weeks.

During that time, they are left to navigate emotional distress on their own.

By the time help becomes available, the moment that led them to seek support has often shifted. Sometimes the urgency has passed. Sometimes the opportunity for reflection has been lost. In some cases, something harmful has already occurred.

This was not always the case.

Before modern systems, people did not wait weeks for help.

They showed up.

They knocked on doors.

They sat at kitchen tables.

They went to neighbors, family members, pastors, and elders.

Help was not scheduled.

It was immediate.

It was relational.

It was integrated into daily life.

This does not mean those systems were perfect. There were gaps, and not everyone received the help they needed.

However, something was present that is often missing today:

Immediate human response.

Through experience, I learned that availability matters.

The most crucial time to be present for someone is not weeks later.

It is in the middle of their need.

When individuals are met in that moment—with presence, stability, and guidance—they are often more open, more aware, and more capable of change.

Research supports this.

Crisis intervention models emphasize immediate response, stabilization, and emotional support during the moment of distress. Studies show that individuals often experience relief during real-time interaction, not after delayed appointments.

Timing is not a minor detail in care.

It is a determining factor in the outcome.

If systems are designed only to respond after distress has escalated or stabilized, they will continue to miss the very moments where intervention is most effective.

Restoring healthy communities requires reestablishing immediate relational access.

Support must be available not only through structured systems, but through people who are present when it matters most.

Preventive Health and Informed Choice

Preventive health reform gives people choices in the services they receive. Healthcare providers educate patients about both treatment and prevention, including the long-term use of medications, lifestyle practices, nutrition, and healthy living. Patients are not simply prescribed solutions; they are educated so they can make informed decisions about their health.

Community hubs also support preventive care.

Gardens, teaching kitchens, and local gathering spaces become places where families learn about food, health, and stewardship of the body.

Mentorship and education strengthen families before problems become medical or institutional crises.

Family Stabilization and Youth Development

Strong communities invest in families and young people. Mentorship programs, community hubs, and youth resources provide guidance and intervention when families are struggling.

Spaces for teens and young adults help develop responsibility, direction, and resilience. Celebration centers recognize achievements such as overcoming obstacles, completing a GED, gaining employment, or reaching personal milestones. When communities celebrate growth, individuals gain hope and motivation to continue moving forward.

Identity Discipleship

Identity must be established before intervention. Churches play an essential role in restoring identity through discipleship, mentorship, and spiritual formation. People must first understand who they are before systems attempt to define what is wrong.

When individuals struggle, communities help determine whether the need is spiritual guidance, mentorship, relational support, or clinical mental health care. Identity, faith, and belonging help stabilize people before institutional systems become the primary response.

Restoring The Role of Community Counselors

The village restores roles that once belonged to the community. Mentors, elders, and shepherd leaders guide others through wisdom, testimony, and lived experience. These community counselors walk beside individuals and families, helping them navigate life before crisis escalates into institutional intervention.

Institutional Balance and System Reform

Institutions have important roles, but they must operate within their proper boundaries.

Schools educate.

Healthcare treats illness.

Churches disciple.

Communities build belonging.

When these roles are confusing, institutions expand while relationships weaken. Reform restores balance by ensuring that institutions support communities rather than replace them.

Prophetic voices, educators, and community leaders help clarify these roles through teaching, resources, and public conversations that remind society how healthy communities function.

The Goal of the Village

The goal of the village is not to eliminate institutions but to restore the relational foundations that allow people to flourish.

A restored village educates, mentors, disciplines, celebrates, and supports its people.

End Of the Book

Human beings were never meant to face life alone.

Clinical care plays an essential role when minds and bodies become overwhelmed by illness, trauma, or instability. In those moments, trained professionals, medical intervention, and structured treatment saved lives and restored safety.

However, many of the struggles' people face today are not illnesses. They are the consequences of disconnection: fractured families, lost mentorship, weakened communities, and the absence of meaningful belonging.

When those structures disappear, the clinical system becomes the place where people bring every form of pain. However, diagnosis cannot replace identity, medication cannot replace purpose, and therapy cannot replace community.

If we want stronger individuals and healthier societies, we must restore the environments where resilience is formed: families that communicate, mentors who guide, communities that hold people accountable, and relationships where individuals are known and supported.

Clinical care must remain protected for those who truly need stabilization. However, human flourishing will always require something more.

It requires people to walk through life together.

That is where reform begins.

References

Clinical Mental Health and Psychiatry

American Psychiatric Association. (2013).

Diagnostic and statistical manual of mental disorders (5th ed.).

American Psychiatric Association. (2022).

Diagnostic and statistical manual of mental disorders (5th ed., text rev.; DSM-5-TR).

Frances, A. (2013). *Saving normal.* HarperCollins.

Insel, T. (2010). Rethinking mental illness. *Nature.*

Stein, M. B., & Stein, D. J. (2008). Social anxiety disorder. *The Lancet.*

Wakefield, J. C. (1992). The concept of mental disorder. *American Psychologist.*

Wakefield, J. C., & First, M. B. (2012). The DSM-5 grief controversy. *World Psychiatry.*

Whisman, M. A., & Beach, S. R. H. (2001). Marital discord and depression. *Clinical Psychology Review.*

Sociology, Culture, and Community

Conrad, P. (2007). The medicalization of society: On the transformation of human conditions into treatable disorders. Johns Hopkins University Press.

Conrad, P., & Barker, K. (2010). The social construction of illness. Journal of Health and Social Behavior.

Furedi, F. (2004). Therapy culture: Cultivating vulnerability in an uncertain age. Routledge.

Illouz, E. (2008). Saving the modern soul: Therapy, emotions, and the culture of self-help. University of California Press.

Putnam, R. D. (2000). Bowling alone: The collapse and revival of American community. Simon & Schuster.

U.S. Surgeon General. (2023). Our epidemic of loneliness and isolation.

Wells, D. F. (1993). No place for truth. Eerdmans.

Psychology, Development, and Human Behavior

Arnett, J. J. (2005). Emerging adulthood. *American Psychologist*.

Bonanno, G. A. (2004). Loss, trauma, and human resilience. *American Psychologist*.

Cacioppo, J. T., & Cacioppo, S. (2018). Loneliness in the modern age: An evolutionary theory of loneliness. *Advances in Experimental Social Psychology*.

Deci, E. L., & Ryan, R. M. (2000). Intrinsic and extrinsic motivations. *Contemporary Educational Psychology*.

Dweck, C. (2006). *Mindset*. Random House.

Erikson, E. H. (1968). *Identity: Youth and crisis*. Norton.

Kashdan, T. B., & Rottenberg, J. (2010). Psychological flexibility. *Clinical Psychology Review*.

Maslow, A. (1968). *Toward a psychology of being*. Van Nostrand.

Ryff, C. (1989). Happiness is everything, or is it? *Journal of Personality and Social Psychology*.

Siegel, D. J. (2012). *The developing mind*. Guilford Press.

Relationships and Family Systems

Bowen, M. (1978). Family therapy in clinical practice. Jason Aronson.

Canary, D., & Dindia, K. (2013). Communication in relationships. Routledge.

Gottman, J. M. (1999). The seven principles for making marriage work. Crown.

Gottman, J. M., & Levenson, R. W. (1992). Marital processes predictive of dissolution. Journal of Personality and Social Psychology.

Johnson, S. (2004). Emotionally focused couple therapy. Brunner-Routledge.

Addiction, Medication, and Behavioral Patterns

Billioti de Gage, S., et al. (2014). Benzodiazepine use and Alzheimer's risk. *BMJ*.

Islam, M. M., et al. (2016). Benzodiazepine use and dementia risk. *BMC Medicine*.

Schiltenwolf, M., et al. (2014). Opioid therapy and cognitive function. *Pain Physician*.

Schmitz, A. (2016). Benzodiazepine misuse. *Substance Abuse*.

Shih, H. I., et al. (2015). Zolpidem and dementia risk. *Journal of Clinical Psychiatry*.

Winick, C. (1962). Maturing out of narcotic addiction. *Bulletin on Narcotics*.

Adolescence and Youth Development

Casey, B. J., Jones, R. M., & Hare, T. A. (2008). The adolescent brain. *Annals of the New York Academy of Sciences*.

Johnston, L. D., et al. (2023). *Monitoring the future.*

Resnick, M. D., et al. (1997). Protecting adolescents from harm. *JAMA.*

Scales, P. C., & Leffert, N. (2004). *Developmental assets.* Search Institute.

Steinberg, L. (2014). *Age of opportunity.* Houghton Mifflin Harcourt.

Spiritual and Religious Studies

Bible. Acts 2:42–47.

Bible. 2 Timothy 3:1–5.

Smith, C., & Denton, M. L. (2005). *Soul searching: The religious and spiritual lives of American teenagers.* Oxford University Press.

Tan, S. Y. (2011). *Counseling and psychotherapy: A Christian perspective.* Baker Academic.

Johnson, E. L. (2010). *Psychology and Christianity: Five views.* InterVarsity Press.

Public Health, Community, and Preventive Health

Drinkwater, C., Wildman, J., & Moffatt, S. (2019). Social prescribing. *BMJ.*

Hammons, A. J., & Fiese, B. H. (2011). Shared family meals and nutrition. *Pediatrics.*

Holt-Lunstad, J., Smith, T. B., & Layton, J. B. (2010). Social relationships and mortality risk. *PLOS Medicine.*

Harvard T.H. Chan School of Public Health. *Healthy Eating Plate & whole-food nutrition research.*

Columbia University National Center on Addiction and Substance Abuse. *The importance of family dinners.*

World Health Organization. (2004). *Prevention of mental disorders: Effective interventions and policy options.*

Viswanathan, M., et al. (2010). *Outcomes of community health worker interventions.* Agency for Healthcare Research and Quality.

U.S. Surgeon General. (2023). *Our epidemic of loneliness and isolation: The U.S. Surgeon General's advisory on the healing effects of social connection and community.*

Ethics and Professional Standards

American Counseling Association. (2014). *ACA Code of Ethics.*

American Medical Association. (2023). Informed consent in patient–physician interactions.

Beauchamp, T. L., & Childress, J. F. (2019). *Principles of biomedical ethics* (8th ed.). Oxford University Press.

Maslach, C., & Leiter, M. P. (2016). Burnout: A multidimensional perspective